TREASURES & LEGENDS
OF THE BRICKYARD

Since 1976, The Indianapolis Motor Speedway Hall of Fame Museum has played host to racing enthusiasts from all around the world.

Plan to visit the museum on your next trip to the track.
- Open 9 a.m. to 5 p.m. (9 to 6 during May)
- Open 364 days a year
- Admission $2, 16 and under free

THE MOST DIVERSIFIED COLLECTION IN THE WORLD.

HALL of FAME MUSEUM™

4790 West 16th Street · Indianapolis, IN 46222 · (317) 481-8500

BOARD OF DIRECTORS

TONY HULMAN, JR.
1901 - 1977

MARY HULMAN

MARI GEORGE

TONY GEORGE

CONTENTS

PAGE 24

PAGE 97

PAGE 113

Thank You 4
Entry List 6
Trackside Files 10
"500" Festival 44
The 33 Starters 46
For Those Who Tried 84
Before the Roar 88
The 1994 Race 92
Canadian Power 108
Qualifying Awards 114
Special Incentive Awards 115
Contingency Awards 116
USAC and Officials 117
Daily Practice Laps 118
Daily Practice Speeds 120
Qualification Attempt Summary 122
Starting Lineup 123
Interval Scoring 124
Official Box Score 125
Credits 127
Marks of Tradition 128

Published by: Indy 500 Publications, IMS Corporation.
Director: William R. Donaldson
Executive Editor: Kurt D. Hunt
Editor: Dawn M. Bair

Graphic Design: Frederick Jungclaus & Michael Kreffel
Editorial Contributions: Bob Laycock, Jan Shaffer, Gordon Kirby, Mark Robinson, Donald Davidson and Lee Driggers.
© 1994 Indianapolis Motor Speedway Corporation.
All Rights Reserved.

INDY 500 PUBLICATIONS - INDY REVIEW VOLUME 4, 1994

ISBN 1-880526-03-4 Library of Congress ISSN 1059-3179

THANK YOU

There is a tradition and staying power in the Indianapolis 500, and in 1994 two of the greatest names ever to be associated with Speedway competition triumphed in the 78th running of the Greatest Spectacle in Racing. Chronicled in this fourth annual edition of *Indy Review* are the remarkable achievements in 1994 of second-time champion Al Unser, Jr., whose family name now appears nine times on the Borg-Warner trophy. Roger Penske, owner of Al Jr.'s '94 Marlboro Penske Mercedes, added to his record number of Indy wins by celebrating his 10th car owner's victory.

The entire Speedway family is proud to once again offer Indy Review as the official record of this wonderful auto race. We bid a fond and heartfelt farewell to Mario Andretti, who raced in his final "500" this year, and we celebrate the great careers of champions Al Unser and Johnny Rutherford who formally announced their retirements this year.

Thanks to all who, like these great champions, have built the Indianapolis 500 into an event, and a tradition, that lasts.

Sincerely,

Tony George

Tony George
President
Indianapolis Motor Speedway

ENTRY

CAR	DRIVER	CAR NAME	YEAR/CHASSIS/ENGINE	ENTRANT
1	Nigel Mansell	Kmart Texaco Havoline Newman/Haas Racing Lola	94 Lola / Ford Cosworth XB	Newman Haas Racing
1T	Nigel Mansell	Kmart Texaco Havoline Newman/Haas Racing Lola	94 Lola / Ford Cosworth XB	Newman Haas Racing
2	Emerson Fittipaldi	Marlboro Penske Mercedes	94 Penske / Mercedes Benz V8	Penske Racing, Inc.
2T	Emerson Fittipaldi	Marlboro Penske Mercedes	94 Penske / Mercedes Benz V8	Penske Racing, Inc.
3	Paul Tracy	Marlboro Penske Mercedes	94 Penske / Mercedes Benz V8	Penske Racing, Inc.
3T	Paul Tracy	Marlboro Penske Mercedes	94 Penske / Mercedes Benz V8	Penske Racing, Inc.
4	Bobby Rahal	Miller Genuine Draft	94 Lola / Honda Indy V-8	Rahal/Hogan Racing
4T	Bobby Rahal	Miller Genuine Draft	94 Lola / Honda Indy V-8	Rahal/Hogan Racing
5	Raul Boesel	Duracell Charger	94 Lola / Ford Cosworth XB	Dick Simon Racing, Inc.
5T	Raul Boesel	Duracell Charger	Lola / Ford Cosworth XB	Dick Simon Racing, Inc.
6	Mario Andretti	Kmart Texaco Havoline Newman/Haas Racing Lola	94 Lola / Ford Cosworth XB	Newman Haas Racing
6T	Mario Andretti	Kmart Texaco Havoline Newman/Haas Racing Lola	94 Lola / Ford Cosworth XB	Newman Haas Racing
7	Adrian Fernandez	Tecate/Quaker State/Reynard/Ilmor	94 Reynard / Ilmor Indy V8/D	Galles Racing International
7T	Adrian Fernandez	Tecate/Quaker State/Reynard/Ilmor	94 Reynard / Ilmor Indy V8/D	Galles Racing International
8	Michael Andretti	Target/Scotch Video Racing	94 Reynard / Ford Cosworth XB	Chip Ganassi Racing Teams Inc.
8T	Michael Andretti	Target/Scotch Video Racing	94 Reynard / Ford Cosworth XB	Chip Ganassi Racing Teams Inc.
9	Robby Gordon	Valvoline Cummins Ford	94 Lola / Ford Cosworth XB	Walker Racing
9T	Robby Gordon	Valvoline Cummins Ford	94 Lola / Ford Cosworth XB	Walker Racing
10	Mike Groff	Motorola	94 Lola / Honda Indy V-8	Rahal/Hogan Racing
10T	Mike Groff	Motorola	94 Lola / Honda Indy V-8	Rahal/Hogan Racing
11	Teo Fabi	Pennzoil Special	94 Reynard 94I / Ilmor Indy V8/D	Hall Racing, Inc.
11T	Teo Fabi	Pennzoil Special	94 Reynard 94I / Ilmor Indy V8/D	Hall Racing, Inc.
12	Jacques Villeneuve	Player's LTD Reynard	94 Reynard / Ford Cosworth XB	Forsythe/Green Racing, Inc.
12T	Jacques Villeneuve	Player's LTD Reynard	94 Reynard / Ford Cosworth XB	Forsythe/Green Racing, Inc.
14	Bryan Herta	AJ Foyt Copenhagen Racing	94 Lola / Ford Cosworth XB	A.J. Foyt Enterprises
15	Mark Smith	Craftsman Tool Ford	94 Lola / Ford Cosworth XB	Walker Racing
15T	Mark Smith	Craftsman Tool Ford	93 Lola / Ford Cosworth XB	Walker Racing
16	Stefan Johansson	Alumax Aluminum	93 Penske / Ilmor Indy V8/D	Bettenhausen Motorsports

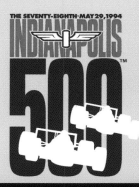

THE SEVENTY-EIGHTH·MAY 29, 1994
INDIANAPOLIS 500™

CAR	DRIVER	CAR NAME	YEAR/CHASSIS/ENGINE	ENTRANT
16T	Stefan Johansson	Alumax Aluminum	93 Penske / Ilmor Indy V8/D	Bettenhausen Motorsports
17	Dominic Dobson	TBA	94 Lola / Ford Cosworth XB	PacWest Racing Group
17T	Dominic Dobson	TBA	94 Lola / Ford Cosworth XB	PacWest Racing Group
18	Jimmy Vasser	Conseco-STP	94 Reynard / Ford Cosworth XB	Hayhoe Racing, Inc.
18T	Jimmy Vasser	Conseco-STP	94 Reynard / Ford Cosworth XB	Hayhoe Racing, Inc.
19	Brian Till	The MI-Jack Car	93 Lola / Ford Cosworth XB	Dale Coyne Racing
19T	TBA	TBA	93 Lola / Ford Cosworth XB	Dale Coyne Racing
21	Roberto Guerrero	Interstate Batteries/Pagan Racing	92 Lola / Buick Indy V6	Pagan Racing, Inc.
21T	Roberto Guerrero	Interstate Batteries/Pagan Racing	92 Lola / Buick Indy V6	Pagan Racing, Inc.
22	Hiro Matsushita	Panasonic Duskin Lola Ford	94 Lola / Ford Cosworth XB	Dick Simon Racing, Inc.
22T	Hiro Matsushita	Panasonic Duskin Lola Ford	Lola / Ford Cosworth XB	Dick Simon Racing, Inc.
23	Buddy Lazier	Financial World	93 Lola / Ilmor Indy V8/C	Leader Cards, Inc.
23T	Buddy Lazier	TBA	TBA / TBA	Leader Cards, Inc.
24	Willy T. Ribbs	Service Merchandise Ford	94 Lola / Ford Cosworth XB	Walker Racing
24T	Willy T. Ribbs	Service Merchandise Ford	93 Lola / Ford Cosworth XB	Walker Racing
25	Marco Greco	TBA	94 Lola / Ford Cosworth XB	Arciero Project Indy
25T	Marco Greco	TBA	93 Lola / Ford Cosworth XB	Arciero Project Indy
26	TBA	TBA	92 Lola / Ford Cosworth XB	Hayhoe Racing, Inc.
27	Eddie Cheever	Quaker State Special	93 Lola / Menard V6	Team Menard, Inc.
27T	Eddie Cheever	Quaker State Special	93 Lola / Menard V6	Team Menard, Inc.
28	Arie Luyendyk	Indy Regency Racing-Eurosport	94 Lola / Ilmor Indy V8/D	Indy Regency Racing
28T	Arie Luyendyk	Indy Regency Racing-Eurosport	94 Lola / Ilmor Indy V8/D	Indy Regency Racing
29	Arie Luyendyk	Indy Regency Racing-Eurosport	92 Lola / Ilmor Indy V8/D	Indy Regency Racing
30	Pancho Carter	Alfa Laval/Tetra Pak McCormack Motorsports	93 Lola / Ilmor Indy V8/C	McCormack Motorsports, Inc.
31	Al Unser, Jr.	Marlboro Penske Mercedes	94 Penske / Mercedes Benz V8	Penske Racing, Inc.
31T	Al Unser, Jr.	Marlboro Penske Mercedes	94 Penske / Mercedes Benz V8	Penske Racing, Inc.
33	John Andretti	Jonathan Byrds Cafeteria Bryant Heating & Cooling	94 Lola / Ford Cosworth XB	Jonathan Byrd/A.J. Foyt Racing
34	TBA	TBA	94 Lola / Ford Cosworth XB	Tasman Motorsports Group, Inc.
35	Fredrik Ekblom	Alfa Laval/Tetra Pak McCormack Motorsports	93 Lola / Ilmor Indy V8/C	McCormack Motorsports, Inc.

ENTRY

CAR	DRIVER	CAR NAME	YEAR/CHASSIS/ENGINE	ENTRANT
36	Stephan Gregoire	Formula Project 500 Babyback's France Info	92 Lola / Buick V6	Formula Project 500 Inc.
36T	Stephan Gregoire	Formula Project 500 Babyback's France Info	TBA / TBA	Formula Project 500 Inc.
38	TBA	Pennzoil Special	94 Reynard / Ilmor Indy V8/D	Hall Racing, Inc.
39	Ross Bentley	The AGFA Car	93 Lola / Ford Cosworth XB	Dale Coyne Racing
40	Scott Goodyear	Budweiser King	94 Lola / Ford Cosworth XB	Kenny Bernstein's Budweiser King Racing
40T	Scott Goodyear	Budweiser King	94 Lola / Ford Cosworth XB	Kenny Bernstein's Budweiser King Racing
41	TBA	AJ Foyt Copenhagen Racing	93 Lola / Ford Cosworth XB	A.J. Foyt Enterprises
42	Michael Greenfield	Greenfield Industries-Lola	93 Lola / Greenfield GC 209T	Greenfield Competition Services,Inc
42T	Michael Greenfield	Greenfield Industries-Lola	Lola / Greenfield GC 209T	Greenfield Competition Services,Inc
44	Al Unser	TBA	94 Lola / Ford Cosworth XB	Arizona Motor-Sport Racing
44T	Al Unser	TBA	93 Lola / Ford Cosworth XB	Arizona Motor-Sport Racing
45	John Paul, Jr.	Pro Formance Team Losi XX	93 Lola / Ilmor Indy V8/D	Pro Formance Motorsports
46	TBA	Pro Formance Team Losi XX	93 Lola / Ilmor Indy V8/D	Pro Formance Motorsports
48	John Andretti	Jonathan Byrds Cafeteria Bryant Heating & Cooling	93 Lola / Ford Cosworth XB	Jonathan Byrd/A.J. Foyt Racing
50	Jeff Andretti	Agip-Gillette-Hawaiian Tropic-Euromotoroils-Epson	93 Lola / Ilmor Indy V8/C+	Euromotorsport Racing, Inc.
50T	Jeff Andretti	Agip-Gillette-Hawaiian Tropic-Euromotoroils-Epson	93 Lola / Ilmor Indy V8/C+	Euromotorsport Racing, Inc.
51	Gary Bettenhausen	Glidden/Menard Special	92 Lola / Menard V6	Team Menard, Inc.
51T	Gary Bettenhausen	Glidden/Menard Special	93 Lola / Menard V6	Team Menard, Inc.
54	TBA	TBA	92 Lola / TBA	Sinden Racing Service Inc.
55	Alessandro Zampedri	Agip-dinema-HEROFLON-itap FLUORIL EUROPA-tau Marin	93 Lola / Ilmor Indy V8/C+	Euromotorsport Racing, Inc.
59	Scott Brayton	Glidden Special	93 Lola / Menard V6	Team Menard, Inc.
59T	Scott Brayton	Glidden Special	93 Lola / Menard V6	Team Menard, Inc.
60	TBA	Budweiser King	93 Lola / Ford Cosworth XB	Kenny Bernstein's Budweiser King Racing
61	TBA	TBA	93 Penske / Ilmor Indy V8/D	Bettenhausen Motorsports

CAR	DRIVER	CAR NAME	YEAR/CHASSIS/ENGINE	ENTRANT
64	TBA	Project Indy/Marcelo Group	94 Lola / Ford Cosworth XB	Project Indy, Inc.
64T	TBA	Project Indy/Marcelo Group	93 Lola / Ford Cosworth XB	Project Indy, Inc.
66	Rocky Moran	Burns Adcox Motor Sports	92 Galmer / Ilmor Indy V8/C+	Burns Adcox Motor Sports
67	Tero Palmroth	Burns Adcox Motor Sports	93 Lola / Ford Cosworth XB	Burns Adcox Motor Sports
68	Johnny Parsons	Burns Adcox Motor Sports	93 Lola / Ford Cosworth XB	Burns Adcox Motor Sports
71	Scott Sharp	TBA	94 Lola / Ford Cosworth XB	PacWest Racing Group
71T	Scott Sharp	TBA	94 Lola / Ford Cosworth XB	PacWest Racing Group
74	Jim Crawford	TBA	91 Lola / Buick V6	Riley & Scott Inc.
74T	Jim Crawford	TBA	92 Lola / Buick V6	Riley & Scott Inc.
76	Tony Bettenhausen	TBA	93 Penske / Ilmor Indy V8/D	Bettenhausen Motorsports
79	Dennis Vitolo	TBA	93 Lola / Ford Cosworth XB	Dick Simon Racing
79T	Dennis Vitolo	TBA	Lola / Ford Cosworth XB	Dick Simon Racing
81	Jeff Wood	Accent On Travel/Pagan Racing	92 Lola / Buick Indy V6	Pagan Racing
84	TBA	AJ Foyt Copenhagen Racing	92 Lola / Ford Cosworth XB	A.J. Foyt Enterprises
85	TBA	TBA	91 Lola / Buick Indy V6	McCormack Motorsports, Inc.
88	Mauricio Gugelmin	Hollywood Indy Car	94 Reynard / Ford Cosworth XB	Chip Ganassi Racing Teams Inc.
89	Michael Andretti	Target/Scotch Video Racing	94 Reynard / Ford Cosworth XB	Chip Ganassi Racing Teams Inc.
90	Lyn St. James	Spirit Of The American Woman-JCPenney/Reebok/Lee	94 Lola / Ford Cosworth XB	Dick Simon Racing, Inc.
90T	Lyn St. James	Spirit Of The American Woman-JCPenney/Reebok/Lee	Lola / Ford Cosworth XB	Dick Simon Racing, Inc.
91	Stan Fox	Delta Faucet-Jack's Tool Rental-Hemelgarn Racing	94 Reynard / Ford Cosworth XB	Hemelgarn Racing, Inc.
94	Didier Theys	Hemelgarn Racing	92 Lola / Buick Indy V6	Hemelgarn Racing, Inc.
95	TBA	Hemelgarn Racing	Lola / Buick Indy V6	Hemelgarn Racing, Inc.
99	Hideshi Matsuda	TBA	Lola / Ford Cosworth XB	Dick Simon Racing, Inc.
99T	Hideshi Matsuda	TBA	Lola / Ford Cosworth XB	Dick Simon Racing, Inc.
102	TBA	Marlboro Penske Mercedes	TBA / TBA	Penske Racing, Inc.
103	TBA	Marlboro Penske Mercedes	TBA / TBA	Penske Racing, Inc.
108	Mario Andretti	Kmart Texaco Havoline Newman/Haas Racing Lola	94 Lola / Ford Cosworth XB	Newman Haas Racing
109	Nigel Mansell	Kmart Texaco Havoline Newman/Haas Racing Lola	94 Lola / Ford Cosworth XB	Newman Haas Racing

The following chronology of the month of May, 1994, was written by Jan Shaffer, Trackside Report editor for the Speedway, and edited by IMS Historian Bob Laycock. The information was compiled under the direction of Bob Walters, IMS Director of Public Relations.

Contributing to this chronicle as the month of May unfolded were Speedway Press Room Manager Bill York and staffers Tim Sullivan, Jack Marsh, Bob Wilson and Charlie Heflin; the Trackside Report team of assistants Kris Callfas, Starre Szelag and Janine Vogrin and staffers Gwynda Eversole, Patty Giudice, Lisa Hall, Ruth Ann Cadou Hoffman, Tony Hoffman, Lucy Jackson, Al Larsen, Becky Lenhard, Vern Morseman, Suzanne Robinson, Victoria Vander Well and historian Bob Watson; and Speedway Computer Services Manager Lee Driggers and assistants Richard Smith and Jeremy Lane.

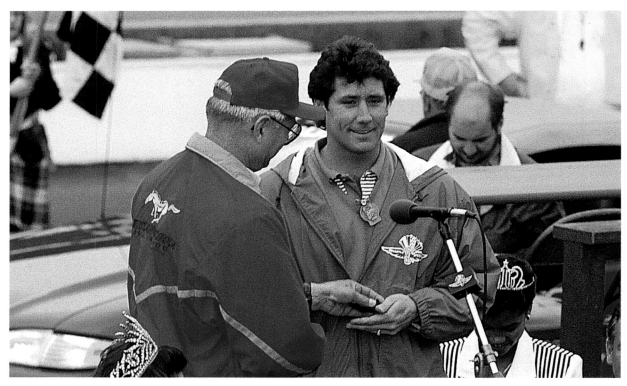

Despite the wet conditions, Speedway President Tony George accepted the ceremonial keys to the pace car, officially opening the track.

Dick Simon's fleet of race cars was ready for Simon's annual "first out" show, but the weather wasn't.

Simon has made an annual production of the honor of being first on the race track for the month of May and has always come up with a new twist of showmanship or two. Unfortunately, the track had its first total opening-day rainout since 1975.

Opening ceremonies took place at Noon as the track started to dry from morning showers. Dan Rivard, director of special vehicle operations for Ford Motor Company, presented the keys to the Ford Mustang Cobra pace car to Speedway President Tony George at 12:26 p.m., signifying the opening of the track.

But wet conditions remained and no cars were on pit road awaiting the green.

About 2 p.m., Simon's team pushed its machines through the Gasoline Alley entrance to pit road. Hiro Matsushita's No. 22 Panasonic Duskin entry was first out and had the premier

10

days at Indy and had the interpreter present as he sat on the pit wall taking in the scene and wondering what was about to happen.

He was told through the interpreter that it was an honor to be "first out" and Simon annually tried to claim the honor. He was asked if he was ready for it.

"Yes, of course," he responded with an excited smile, in perfect English.

Date:	Saturday, May 7
Weather:	Rain, High 60°
Drivers On Track:	0
Cars On Track:	0
Total Laps:	0

Lyn St. James was the one Simon driver who was on pit road in civilian clothes. As the cars were pushed out, a fuel pressure problem was discovered in her machine, which required changing the engine and knocking her out of the friendly competition.

"I was thinking of doing a rain dance so I could come and play, too," she said.

It wasn't known whether St. James did a rain dance, or if she claimed victory from it if she did. But at 2:30 p.m., with the track nearly dry, a slight mist turned to rain again.

For the record, Vitolo was the first to sit down in a race car for the month of May and Greco was the first to don a helmet on pit road.

But at 4 p.m., with rain continuing to fall, the track closed for the day without a single lap turned.

Team Menard (left) stood trackside hoping for a break in the weather while the PacWest crew (below) spent the rainy day in the garage.

spot southward to get the drop on the rest.

He was followed, to the north, by rookie Dennis Vitolo (#79), Raul Boesel (#5), rookie Marco Greco (#25 in an Arciero Project Indy entry associated with Simon) and rookie Hideshi Matsuda (#99, in a Beck Motorsports entry associated with Simon).

Matsuda, who had previously filed reports for a Japanese television station at Indy and had been the last driver to pass a USAC "looksee" driver's test to be approved, was unaware of Simon's opening-day fanfare.

He had needed an interpreter in his scant few

DAY 2
SUNDAY, MAY 8

Right; Dick Simon's fleet was first out for the seventh year in a row.

Top; IMS Chairman of the Board Mari Hulman George and Bryan Herta enjoyed the Special Olympics activities. Bottom; Willy T. Ribbs took time out for a game of softball.

With a rainout on opening day, teams had two days of track action crammed into one on Day #2, history was made and ancillary Speedway activities escalated the pace in earnest.

A total of 39 cars got on the track, breaking the opening-day record of 33 set in 1993. Dick Simon's cars and drivers were ready to try for "first out" honors for the second day in a row. And, with the addition of cars for Lyn St. James and Tero Palmroth to the previous day's offering, they put on a show.

Raul Boesel's engine was first to fire, followed quickly by Hiro Matsushita's. Boesel was first away when Matsushita's engine stalled. Dennis Vitolo dropped in behind Boesel as the cars left pit road, followed by Hideshi Matsuda.

The cars came around in a triangle formation with St. James on the point, a second row of Boesel outside and Matsushita inside and a third row, outside to inside, of Matsuda, Palmroth and Vitolo. Marco Greco, scheduled to be a part of the party, stalled in turn #4 to bring out the caution after one lap.

But it was the seventh straight year that an entry associated with Simon was first out.

"They were all on their own," Simon said. "I told them if they crashed, they were done for the day.

Just 41 minutes into the practice session, Michael Andretti became the first driver to exceed 220 miles an hour with a lap at 221.539 miles an hour in the #8T Target/Scotch Video Racing entry and a special moment in Speedway history occurred.

At the same time as Andretti's lap, Bobby Rahal

took out the #4T Miller Genuine Draft car, officially putting the Honda engine on the track and marking the first time in the history of the Speedway that a Japanese car or engine manufacturer had participated.

Fifty-one minutes later, Paul Tracy took out the #3 Marlboro Penske Mercedes, signifying the first Mercedes appearance at Indianapolis since 1948.

From Andretti firing the first major speed salvo, many took turns at the top of the chart during the day, as 1,733 laps were recorded.

Scott Brayton wound up on top, with a lap at 227.658 miles an hour in the #59 Glidden Special, which included a trap speed of 243 miles an hour...a number Brayton didn't believe.

"I saw the speedometer and never went over 235," he said. "If that's what you're going for is fast time, then someone else better do 243, too."

Eight rookies passed the final observation phase of their driver's tests — Brian Till, Greco, Vitolo, Mauricio Gugelmin, Matsuda, Adrian Fernandez, Jacques Villeneuve and Scott Sharp.

The 14th annual "Save Arnold" Barbecue for Special Olympics was held in the Speedway's flag lot and even with the feverish track activity, many drivers took time to attend. A total of 20 drivers and former drivers served as coaches for the Special Olympians.

"We usually have 15-20 drivers who participate and this may have been a record," said Mari Hulman George, the Speedway chairman who founded the event.

And it was on to Day #3.

Date:	Sunday, May 8
Weather:	Cloudy, High 65°
Drivers On Track:	36
Cars On Track:	39
Total Laps:	1,733

Top Five Drivers of the Day

Car	Driver	Speed
59	Scott Brayton	227.658
21	Roberto Guerrero	225.558
27	Eddie Cheever	223.998
5	Raul Boesel	223.908
8T	Michael Andretti	223.769

QUOTE OF THE DAY:
"You want to drive the car, right?"
A.J. Foyt

TRACKSIDE FILES
DAY 3
MONDAY, MAY 9

Michael Andretti put together boxcar numbers early while working with two cars and a whopping 49 other machines on the track couldn't match them as teams turned up the pace.

Andretti ran both the #8 and #8T Target/Scotch Video Racing entries. Just four minutes after the track opened, he reached 225.547 miles an hour in the #8. Fifteen minutes later, he reached 227.038 and the rest of the competitors shot at that number unsuccessfully for the rest of the day.

"Yes, I knew we could do it (run quick in the morning)," Michael said. "Yesterday, I had a great lap right before I blew the engine, so coming out today, I knew it wouldn't be a problem.

"But more encouraging was the speeds I was running at mid-day," he added. "I did those in the spare car and I was doing 226, so that makes me feel better."

Emerson Fittipaldi showed the strength of the Mercedes engine with a lap at 226.512 in the #2 Marlboro Penske Mercedes and Scott Brayton made the top three for the second day in a row with a lap of 225.926 in the #59T Glidden Special.

A.J. Foyt made it official that rookie Bryan Herta would be at the wheel of his traditional No. 14 entry. Herta had been fastest in USAC's Rookie Orientation program at 218-plus in Foyt's 1993 Lola and had been getting a long look.

When presented with the official form, Foyt turned to Herta and said, "you want to drive the car, right?" Herta nodded and Foyt signed off.

"I think the speeds at first are a little intimidating," Herta said. "That (speed at ROP) was 70 miles an hour faster than I'd ever been in a race car. You definitely have to give the track its respect."

At 4:45 p.m., Mike Groff became the first wall victim of the month, having an apparent

engine problem going into turn #1 and hitting the south chute wall in the #10 Motorola entry. Groff was examined for a bruised left foot, released from Hanna Medical Center and cleared to drive.

"Something rattled in the back of the car going into #1," Groff said. "I thought we had it collected at the exit of #1, but it was just one of those things. There was really no way of saving it."

In all, entries ran 1,815 laps and produced a top 10 drivers' list at more than 221 miles an hour. As speeds rose for many, the pole position picture was becoming increasingly unclear.

Would it be a Mercedes, and what power did the Penske cars really have in the new engine? Would Andretti's new Reynard chassis with a Ford engine be the combination? Or would it be Brayton's Menard powerplant? Or something else altogether?

The next few days would tell.

	Date:	Monday, May 9
	Weather:	Sunny, High 69°
Drivers On Track:		38
Cars On Track:		51
Total Laps:		1,815

Top Five Drivers of the Day

Car	Driver	Speed
8	Michael Andretti	227.038
2	Emerson Fittipaldi	226.512
59T	Scott Brayton	225.926
5	Raul Boesel	225.853
21	Roberto Guerrero	225.739

Top; Mike Groff was the first to greet the wall in 1994. Middle; Rookie Bryan Herta seized the opportunity to drive for A.J. Foyt. Bottom; Michael Andretti walked away with the day's fastest speed.

13

DAY 4
TUESDAY, MAY 10

Raul Boesel

Eddie Cheever

Leaders in the month of May speed derby swapped the top spot around as drivers and teams started to show their hands for Pole Day.

But just as they started to show what they had, the speeds raised many questions as to who might have just a little bit more.

Raul Boesel wound up on top of the heap at 230.403 in the #5 Duracell Charger, turning the lap just five minutes before the track closed for the day. He became the first driver since a group in 1992 to reach the 230-mile-an-hour barrier in practice.

Earlier, Michael Andretti had started fast for the second straight day with a lap of 224.927 just 27 minutes into the practice period.

Boesel countered at 227.244 at 11:50 a.m. Then Mario Andretti got the fastest lap of the month at 228.351 at 12:14 p.m. in the #6 Kmart Texaco Havoline Newman/Haas Racing Lola.

The Penske team then unloaded its guns.

Emerson Fittipaldi put the #2 Marlboro Penske Mercedes on top with a lap at 229.113 at 12:27 p.m. Two minutes later, Paul Tracy reached 229.961 in the #3 Penske machine.

Tracy stayed at the head of the list for more than five hours until Boesel turned heads with the month's fastest lap.

Unexpectedly, Boesel somewhat pooh-poohed the lap, leaving other competitors and the public alike wondering what to make of it.

"I was running speeds of 227 and the car wasn't stable, so we made some changes and went in the right direction," Boesel said. "I don't want to be cocky, but that wasn't a completely clear lap. I didn't think it was that good."

Although Boesel was top gun, the Penskes had shown that the horsepower suspected of the Mercedes powerplant was real. The engine went on the dynamometer in January and was on a track for the first time in February. Even while practicing at Indy for keeps, the team had been using its test team to further develop the engine "on the fly" during early May at Michigan.

In addition, the Penskes were sporting a "Novi-like" tail fin, which had been copied over the last two days by the teams of Michael Andretti, Bobby Rahal and Nigel Mansell.

"Obviously, in the wind tunnel, it's proven to give us some aerodynamic benefit," said team owner Roger Penske at a press conference. "USAC made us cut six inches off of it so it wouldn't be beyond the center line of the rear axle."

Penske wouldn't predict a pole speed.

"Yesterday was the first time we've had all three drivers in their primary cars," he said. "I don't think anybody's run their qualifying setup yet. We might be knocked off the pole. I'm not sure we're going to win the race. But that's where we want to be."

Day #4 was the first in which teams passed 2,000 laps of practice, with 43 cars turning 2,006 circuits of the historic 2 1/2-mile oval.

Bryan Herta and Mark Smith became the ninth and 10th rookies to complete driver's tests.

The drama continued.

	Date:	Tuesday, May 10
	Weather:	Sunny, High 72°
Drivers On Track:		38
Cars On Track:		43
Total Laps:		2,006

Top Five Drivers of the Day

Car	Driver	Speed
5	Raul Boesel	230.403
3	Paul Tracy	229.961
2	Emerson Fittipaldi	229.264
27	Eddie Cheever	228.676
6	Mario Andretti	228.351

QUOTE OF THE DAY:
"We'll see what they can do Saturday."
Nigel Mansell

TRACKSIDE FILES
DAY 5
WEDNESDAY, MAY 11

Speeds waned on this day in the wake of 17 mile-an-hour winds that threw off setups and left some wondering exactly who was where in the pole position scenario.

The gusts also left room for some to speculate on what was left to prove before Pole Day qualifying beckoned.

Al Unser Jr., was fastest of the day at 226.478 in the #31 Marlboro Penske Mercedes after teammate Paul Tracy and Newman/Haas Racing's Mario Andretti and Nigel Mansell had taken turns at the top.

Since speeds were "off," it was a day to ask

n't do it on his own."

Others continued to copy the Penske team's tail fins. Among them were Jacques Villeneuve in the #12 Players LTD Reynard, Adrian Fernandez in the #7 Tecate/Quaker State/Reynard/Ilmor, Mark Smith in the #15 Craftsman Tool Ford and Mario Andretti in the #6 Kmart Texaco Havoline Newman/Haas Racing Lola.

The "fin frenzy" quickly caught the eye of sponsor representatives. "They'll make good billboards," one said.

Al Unser, Jr.

Unser Jr., if the Penske team was "sandbagging" or not.

"The Marlboro Penske car is not a lock for the pole," Unser Jr. said. "We need to get the car around the corners to go quick. We're still fighting the car for handling."

In a press briefing, Mansell didn't think the Penske team's "fight" was all that much of a struggle.

"I think the Penskes are probably only using about 50 inches of boost," Mansell said. "I think they're saving five inches of boost for Saturday. We'll see what they can do on Saturday but they're going to be very quick."

Mansell also said that Raul Boesel got some help on his 230-mile-an-hour-plus lap the previous day.

"Did you watch the lap?," he asked. "He was perfectly positioned on the track to be behind two or three cars so he got sucked up the straights. Don't get me wrong, it was a great lap, but he did-

Date:	Wednesday, May 11	
Weather:	Sunny, Windy, High 76°	
Drivers On Track:	37	
Cars On Track:	42	
Total Laps:	1,376	

Top Five Drivers of the Day

Car	Driver	Speed
31	Al Unser, Jr.	226.478
1	Nigel Mansell	225.807
6	Mario Andretti	225.519
8	Michael Andretti	224.949
3	Paul Tracy	224.433

With 10 rookies already through drivers' tests, only two — Ross Bentley and Fredrik Ekblom — remained to complete their tests for USAC's final approval.

Dale Coyne, fielding a car for Bentley, said his driver would wait until after the first qualifying weekend to finish off the exam. A spokesman for McCormack Motorsports, which had entered Ekblom, said the team's priority was to get veteran Pancho Carter in the field before turning its attention to Ekblom, who had yet to take the track although he had passed four phases of the driver's test during USAC's Rookie Orientation Program.

Unser Jr., had been splitting his time between Indy and testing at Michigan.

"The Mercedes gets better and better," he said. "It's been really, really good having been running up there. It has helped us coming here."

And in the wind, at least, he was top gun.

Top; Team Penske started a fad with their newly-designed tail fin. Bottom; Speedway Historian Bob Laycock kept the Press Room running smoothly during the month.

Above; Mario Andretti hoped to repeat his 1969 win in his last go around at Indy. Right; Four-time winner Al Unser had his hands full with his inexperienced team.

Some new names appeared at the top of the speed chart for varying periods of time on this day, just 48 hours before pole qualifying.

First, Eddie Cheever hit 223.153 in the #27 Quaker State Special just five minutes after the Speedway opened for practice. Michael Andretti pushed it to 225.637, then Robby Gordon, for the first time, took a day's top spot at 226.946 in the #9 Valvoline Cummins Ford.

Gordon stayed in the No. 1 spot for nearly an hour before the Penske team unloaded its weapons.

Emerson Fittipaldi and Paul Tracy started exchanging the lead, with Fittipaldi becoming the second driver of the month to exceed 230 with successive laps of 230.055 and 230.438, the last coming at 5:23 p.m.

Both Fittipaldi and Tracy had trap speeds of 244 miles an hour, with winds of only 10 miles an hour. But Fittipaldi said the winds helped, when a day earlier, they had held down speeds.

"I think the wind helped determine my speed today," Fittipaldi said. "It was much faster coming out of (turn) #4. I did it myself. I didn't have a draft. The way the car handled today was much, much better than two days ago."

As usual, he was asked about "sandbagging," although to most it created wonder about how a driver might sandbag with a 230-mile-an-hour lap.

"No way, we're not sandbagging," Fittipaldi exclaimed. "I don't see the advantage. People don't realize that there's no advantage to it."

A whopping 44 cars took the track to run the month of May's biggest one-day total of practice laps with 2,416.

Meanwhile, both Mario Andretti and Al Unser held media briefings in the Trackside Conference Room. Andretti is on what is billed as the "Arriverderci Tour," his retirement already announced for the end of the 1994 season. This was to be his last Indianapolis 500.

"For quite some years, the question was always popping up, 'when are you going to retire?,'" Andretti said. "I think when I was 50 in age...I don't feel any different but let's be realistic. I felt every year from there on would be a bonus. I

used to think about it in five-year sections, then it started being year-to-year.

"I have to be honest with myself," he added. "I'm not as quick as I used to be but I'm quick enough to be involved, to be a factor."

Of the five days of running in the 1994 month of May to date, Andretti had been in the top 10 in all five and third on Day #5.

	Date:	Thursday, May 12
	Weather:	Sunny, High 73°
Drivers On Track:		40
Cars On Track:		44
Total Laps:		2,416

Top Five Drivers of the Day		
Car	Driver	Speed
2	Emerson Fittipaldi	230.438
3	Paul Tracy	228.444
8T	Michael Andretti	227.698
31	Al Unser, Jr.	227.457
5	Raul Boesel	227.175

Unser also talked about retirement, and what would help make his decision.

"The day I wake up and say, 'it's not fun' or 'I'm not competitive' is different," Unser said. "But I still enjoy it and here I am."

The four-time "500" winner was asked about his reputation of taking care of equipment.

"I wish I could say there's a technique to making the car last but I can't," Unser said. "You never exactly know. I wish I could come up with all the answers on that and we wouldn't hafta race."

Emerson Fittipaldi

QUOTE OF THE DAY:
"It all depends on how much bluff there is out there."
Derrick Walker

TRACKSIDE FILES
DAY 7
FRIDAY, MAY 13

It was the day before Pole Day and all through the garage, everyone was stirring about the Penske barrage.

The Penske team's Mercedes engine had put a hex on everyone else. Some even felt it was capable of 260 miles an hour, a figure team owner Roger Penske had termed 'absolutely out of the ball park" a few days earlier.

But no one, not even those with the Penske team, knew what the pole speed would be. Weather and the Mercedes were both unknowns on the final day of practice before the No. 1 starting position would be decided.

"It all depends on how much bluff there is out there," said Derrick Walker, owner of cars driven by Robby Gordon, Willy T. Ribbs and Mark Smith. "Realistically, maybe a 235, 236 as maximum top speed."

The rest of the pack quickly put up numbers.

Ten minutes after the track opened, Mario Andretti hit 224.338. It stayed at the top just nine minutes before Gordon reached 225.587. Three minutes later, Michael Andretti reeled off a lap at 226.068. That was best for only two minutes, then Nigel Mansell took over at 226.895.

Then came the Penskes.

Left; A young fan watched the action on the track in amazement.

Paul Tracy

Nigel Mansell

Right; Emerson Fittipaldi found time to spend with his children between hot laps on the track.

Paul Tracy put the #3 Marlboro Penske Mercedes at the head of the list nine minutes after Mansell's lap with a circuit of 228.114 before Fittipaldi hit 230-plus for the second straight day 43 minutes later at 230.138. And nobody touched him the rest of the day.

Even with Fittipaldi's hot lap, things weren't 100 percent sweet for the Penske forces.

At 3:37 p.m., Tracy did 1 1/2 spins through turn #3, shot through the grass and whacked the outside wall in turn #4. The car made a second contact, then spun across the track to the inside guard rail.

Top left; P.A. Announcer Tom Carnegie revealed the qualifying order for Pole Day. Top right; Robby Gordon, John Andretti and Bryan Herta talked shop on pit road. Bottom; Paul Tracy sent his car to the body shop and himself to the hospital after making contact in turn #4.

Tracy was transported to Methodist Hospital, where he was treated for a concussion and a bruised left foot and admitted in good condition. His clearance to drive on Pole Day was questionable.

Later, Smith brushed the wall in the north short chute, but drove it back to the pits with minor suspension damage.

Although 46 cars took the track, no one could touch Fittipaldi, who turned his hottest lap at 12:16 p.m. on a day when conditions were optimum...a high of 71 degrees and winds at only eight miles an hour.

He was asked if his teammates would be his biggest competition for the pole.

"Yes," he replied cautiously. "Nigel... Michael... Mario...Raul has been strong."

Tero Palmroth, who had been in a car only for Dick Simon's opening-day "first out" production, was officially named to drive Simon's #79T entry, the backup to Dennis Vitolo.

The pole awaited.

Date:	Friday, May 13
Weather:	Sunny, High 71°
Drivers On Track:	40
Cars On Track:	46
Total Laps:	2,372

Top Five Drivers of the Day

Car	Driver	Speed
2	Emerson Fittipaldi	230.138
3	Paul Tracy	228.693
6	Mario Andretti	227.618
8T	Michael Andretti	227.589
31	Al Unser, Jr.	227.359

19

Rookie Hideshi Matsuda was first in line when qualifying opened at 12:15 p.m. He had been a Japanese television commentator previously at the Speedway and was in the #99 Dick Simon-prepared machine for Beck Motorsports.

He had been the last of the 25 drivers to post his quickest speed of the month in the morning practice, with a lap at 222.629.

Matsuda put together four laps at an average speed of 222.545, setting one- and four-lap records for rookies in the process. His single fastest lap of 222.646 broke Robby Gordon's 1993 mark of 222.563 and his four-lap average broke Jimmy Vasser's 1992 standard of 222.313.

As the line progressed, some were ready and some were not. Eddie Cheever jumped in next at 223.163 in the #27 Quaker State Special, but Scott Brayton waved off after three laps in the 221 bracket. The elements of rain, the line and the speed to make the field were magnified as crews were forced to make decisions based on all three.

Dominic Dobson was next and registered an average of 222.970 in the #17 PacWest Racing Group entry. Scott Goodyear then waved off before Raul Boesel put up numbers for the field to see.

Boesel had been fast all month and qualified the #5 Duracell Charger at 227.618.

"I enjoy this place very well," Boesel said. "(The fans) have been a lot more supportive this year.

Above; Rookie Hideshi Matsuda cruised easily through four laps to become the first qualifier of 1994. Right; Al Unser Jr. proved to the world that the Mercedes was for real.

Cool temperatures greeted drivers and teams as they prepared to chase the $100,000 PPG Pole Award and other qualifying prizes, but one driver would not be involved.

Paul Tracy, who had suffered a concussion a day earlier, was released from Methodist Hospital but not cleared to drive, leaving the Penske team with the Mercedes-powered machines of Emerson Fittipaldi and Al Unser Jr. to join the hunt.

With a temperature of 59 degrees as the 8 a.m. practice started, 25 drivers posted their fastest speeds of the month, led by Nigel Mansell's 228.137 and teammate Mario Andretti's 228.606. But the practice didn't last long. Rain halted it at 9:34 a.m., after 44 cars had run a total of 778 laps.

Lyn St. James

Raul Boesel

Many of them have told me that 'we hope you can do it this year because the Speedway owes you one.' This morning, I thought I had a shot at the pole. I was relaxed and the car was very good."

After a waveoff by Adrian Fernandez, rookie Dennis Vitolo qualified at 222.439 and his fast lap of 222.954 broke the rookie one-lap mark set earlier by Matsuda.

Then came Michael Andretti, who put the #8 Target/Scotch Video Racing entry in the show for Chip Ganassi at 226.205.

Robby Gordon waved off and Jacques Villeneuve was next.

Villeneuve had just come away from an accident at Phoenix and had had an impressive rookie month at Indy with the new Reynard chassis.

His fastest lap of 227.061 and average

21

Jacques Villeneuve

Right; The Penske cheering section went nuts when Al Jr. recorded the fastest speed of the day.

of 226.259 bested the records set earlier by Vitolo and Matsuda for rookie drivers as the class of '94 continued to be impressive.

At 1:18 p.m., Al Unser Jr. rolled away for his run, the first of the Penske drivers to show what they had.

His first lap was only 225.722 miles an hour, but the next two were in the 228 bracket and the fourth was his fastest at 229.481 for an average of 228.011, fastest of the day.

"I got caught in the rain this morning during practice going for 229 and I almost crashed, which scared the you-know-what out of me," Unser Jr. said. "So, I was building my speed back up. During the qualifying run, when I saw the 225, I thought, 'oh, man, I need to go after it.' And I did. The Mercedes ran great."

Teo Fabi waved off before Mike Groff put the #10T Motorola Lola Honda machine in at 218.808, the first qualifier to take a speed below 220 miles an hour.

"We've lost three, four, five engines this week,"

Groff said. "It's put us back a lot. We were out there running flat out. We've got to go back to the drawing board."

His Rahal-Hogan teammate, Bobby Rahal, was next in the #4 Miller Genuine Draft entry and did little better at 220.178.

Arie Luyendyk qualified at 223.673 in the #28 Indy Regency Racing-Eurosport machine, Nigel Mansell got the #1 Kmart Texaco Havoline Newman/Haas Racing Lola in the show at 224.041 and Stan Fox put in the #91 Delta Faucet-Jack's Tool Rental-Hemelgarn Racing car at 222.867 before rain halted qualifying for two hours, 59 minutes.

When the track reopened at 4:58 p.m., just an hour and two minutes remained in the day's qualifying activities. It would be a fast flurry as eight drivers blasted their way into the show around five waveoffs.

Rookie Scott Sharp qualified at 222.091 to lead the charge in the #71 PacWest Racing Group Lola. Then came John Andretti, who was trying to

with an average of 220.460 in the #88 Hollywood Indy Car.

Roberto Guerrero checked in at 221.278 in the #21 Interstate Batteries/Pagan Racing machine to become the day's 20th qualifier.

After Marco Greco waved off, Hiro Matsushita qualified the #22 Panasonic Duskin Lola Ford at 221.382 as the gun sounded.

Left in the qualifying line, and still with a chance at the pole on Sunday, were Mario Andretti, Robby Gordon and Emerson Fittipaldi. Unser Jr. would need to wait a day to find out if he got his first "500" pole.

Left; Rookie Mauricio Gugelmin found a place to relax in the midst of the action.

become the first driver ever to run the Indianapolis 500 and Coca Cola 600 stock car race at Charlotte, N.C., on the same day.

He put the #33 Jonathan Byrd's Cafeteria/ Bryant Heating and Cooling car out of the Foyt-Byrd stable in the race at 223.263.

Lyn St. James went out to make history at the Speedway once again. Her run was consistent, with a top lap of 224.282 and a slowest lap of 224.070 for a four-lap average of 224.154. It was faster than many accomplished veterans and many talked about the fact that she was faster than Mansell.

"It feels really good," St. James said. "(Mansell) has a great sense of humor and he knows he's going to get razzed. I know I came closer to the wall than I have all week. The emotions came back when I drove into the pits after qualifying and saw my crew members and even some competitors congratulating me."

She had broken her own one- and four-lap Speedway qualifying records for a woman at Indy and wound up fifth in the provisional lineup at the time. She seemed an odds-on choice to start higher than any woman to make the "500" field, the best previous starting spot being 14th by Janet Guthrie in 1979.

Of the next four drivers in line, only rookie Brian Till took his run, averaging 221.107 in the #19 Mi-Jack Car as John Paul Jr., Brayton (in a second car) and Al Unser waved off.

Rookie Bryan Herta was next in the #14 AJ Foyt Copenhagen Racing Lola and recorded a four-lap average of 220.992. His first-lap speed of 218.289 was the 2,000th qualification lap of more than 200 miles an hour at Indy.

With 21 minutes to go, the pole would be decided by the fastest speed on the first day. The qualifying line had been broken as teams jockeyed after the rain delay to get the best possible run at it.

After Teo Fabi waved off for the second time of the day in a backup car, Mauricio Gugelmin became the seventh rookie of the day to qualify

John Andretti

Date:	Saturday, May 14
Weather:	Rain, High 69°
Qualification Attempts:	31
Qualifiers:	21

Pole Day Qualifiers

Car	Driver	Speed
31	Al Unser, Jr.	228.011
5	Raul Boesel	227.618
12	Jacques Villeneuve	226.259
8	Michael Andretti	226.205
90	Lyn St. James	224.154
1	Nigel Mansell	224.041
28	Arie Luyendyk	223.673
33	John Andretti	223.263
27	Eddie Cheever	223.163
17	Dominic Dobson	222.970
91	Stan Fox	222.867
99	Hideshi Matsuda	222.545
79	Dennis Vitolo	222.439
71	Scott Sharp	222.091
22	Hiro Matsushita	221.382
21	Roberto Guerrero	221.278
19	Brian Till	221.107
14	Bryan Herta	220.992
88	Mauricio Gugelmin	220.460
4	Bobby Rahal (Withdrawn 5/21)	220.178
10T	Mike Groff (Withdrawn 5/21)	218.808

Top; Scott Goodyear's luck ran out when disaster struck in the fourth turn. Bottom; Al Unser, Jr. and Roger Penske could only sit and hope Al's pole speed wouldn't be beaten.

Only eight cars remained in the original qualifying order with a shot at the pole, but with Mario Andretti and Emerson Fittipaldi among them, the amassed were more than curious to see what would happen and if Al Unser Jr. could fend off Andretti and his Penske teammate while sitting in the barn.

Again, a wet race track delayed practice until 11:25 a.m., and competitors had only until 12:08 p.m. to make final preparations for a time trial run.

Andretti was first out for the final "500" qualifying attempt of his career, having announced he would retire at the end of the season.

He recorded a four-lap average of 223.503 as the 22nd qualifier of the month of May. He disavowed thoughts of his last run at Indy.

"I don't think of it now," he said. "I need to collect my thoughts now and think about it alone in my office. I can shut everything off. I'll reminisce later. I'm here to do a job and not be concerned about my emotions."

He talked about drawing far down the list, changing weather conditions and the luck and trickiness of both.

"It's not that bad," he said. "I'm not 55th. The draw is not that good. What am I supposed to do, shoot the messenger? This is a game of chance. It used to be that the low numbers meant cool weather. There is so much difference in the conditions themselves. But everyone is meeting the same conditions. What can you do?"

After Andretti, Scott Goodyear (again) and Willy T. Ribbs waved off, bringing Robby Gordon and the #9T Valvoline Cummins Ford to the line. He became the 23rd qualifier at 221.293 in his backup car.

"I'm disappointed," he said. "I know the heat

Teo Fabi

Robby Gordon

was a factor and I'm not happy with 221. This car isn't up to speed yet. We can still qualify the #9 car today and we may do that. Yesterday, the high was 62 degrees and it's already at 78 degrees today."

Stefan Johansson waved off and Brayton came up again. This, Brayton's third attempt in two different cars, was waved off after one lap at 223.021. Clearly, the team expected more.

Jimmy Vasser put the #18 Conseco-STP machine in the field at 222.262 before Fittipaldi came to the line with the final shot to knock Unser Jr. off the pole.

He came up just short,

25

Stefan Johansson

at 227.303 in the #2 Marlboro Penske Mercedes and Unser Jr., had the first "500" pole of his career.

With it came car owner Roger Penske's 11th pole at Indy. Unser Jr., and his father became the first father and son ever to sit on the pole at Indy. He became the third Unser to sit on the pole. And he became the second second-generation driver to qualify on the pole, succeeding Pancho Carter.

Fittipaldi said the change in temperature was critical.

"I was much faster yesterday but the weather is very different today, much more humid today," Fittipaldi said. "Right before I went out, Jr. tells me, 'It is beautiful today, lot of sunshine, real nice and warm for you, Emerson.' The weather was a little against me, but that's racing. Jr. is on the pole and I am third. I'm happy to be on the front row."

Two cars remained in line at that point, and

Paul Tracy took the track to try to become the fastest so-called "second-day" qualifier. He had been cleared to drive earlier in the morning, but he waved off after three laps.

Rookie Adrian Fernandez was next and put together a consistent run in the #7T Tecate/Quaker State/Reynard/Ilmor at 222.657. Tracy came back 59 minutes later to soldier into the field in the #31T Marlboro Penske Mercedes at 222.710.

From then on, it was a wait for cooler temperatures.

Scott Goodyear continued his frustrating month, slamming the wall at 4:20 p.m. in turn #4 and taking a trip to Methodist Hospital for examination of back and left thigh pain. The car sustained heavy left-side damage.

At 4:53 p.m., Teo Fabi and the crew of the #11 Pennzoil Special pushed into line. Fabi had tried both of the team's cars on the previous day but

couldn't get up to speed.

But he recorded a healthy four-lap average of 223.394 to become the 28th qualifier.

He said he had popoff valve problems on Saturday.

"During qualifying, my first lap was 220 and my second lap was 222," he said. "During both laps, my valve wouldn't close. I finally managed to lose it at the end of the second lap when Jim Hall waved me in. It was a very difficult day. I had a good car and expected something good to happen."

After Fabi came John Paul Jr., who waved off. Then Brayton made another try and took the run, averaging 223.652 in the #27T Quaker State Special, a backup car to teammate Eddie Cheever.

"I'm happy to be in the field after four times," he said. "I'm relieved. My first lap was the quickest and I cooked the tires on that lap."

Stefan Johansson was the last of the day to make the field at 221.518 in the #16 Alumax Aluminum entry from Bettenhausen Motorsports only eight minutes before the close of qualifying.

Buddy Lazier took a stab but mustered only two laps in the 218 bracket with three minutes to go.

The field had 30 qualifiers for the weekend. Goodyear was released from Methodist at 7 p.m. and he would be among those who would wait until the final weekend to make their bids to join the field for the 78th Indianapolis 500.

Al Unser, Jr. ran away with the pole and the $100,000 PPG Pole Award check.

	Date:	Sunday, May 15
	Weather:	Sunny, High 75°
Qualification Attempts:	16	
	Qualifiers:	9

Pole Day Qualifiers

Car	Driver	Speed
2	Emerson Fittipaldi	227.303
6	Mario Andretti	223.503
9T	Robby Gordon	221.293
18	Jimmy Vasser	222.262

Day Two Qualifiers

Car	Driver	Speed
27T	Scott Brayton	223.652
11	Teo Fabi	223.394
31T	Paul Tracy	222.710
7T	Adrian Fernandez	222.657
16	Stefan Johansson	221.518

DAY 10
MONDAY, MAY 16

Pancho Carter

Top left; Chief Starter Duane Sweeney directed traffic from his perch. Bottom; Gary Bettenhausen hoped to start his 22nd "500."

After the flurry of qualifying activity, the second week started with many teams taking a day off, some to unwind after qualifying and some to postpone the pressures that were still ahead.

Not Robby Gordon.

The second-year Indy driver held the second, third and fourth spots on the speed chart in three different cars as he helped his Walker Racing teammates sort out their machines as well as his own.

Gordon reached 224.781 in his qualified car, the #9 Valvoline Cummins Ford, 221.965 in the #24 Service Merchandise Ford assigned to Willy T. Ribbs and 221.943 in the #15 Craftsman Tool Ford of Mark Smith.

After 30 cars qualified over the weekend, only three not-yet-qualified drivers were on the track and none were up to comfortable speeds to make the field.

Jim Crawford reached only 210.482, Smith

Date:	Monday, May 16
Weather:	Cloudy, High 66°
Drivers On Track:	15
Cars On Track:	18
Total Laps:	603

Top Non-Qualified Drivers of the Day

Car	Driver	Speed
15	Mark Smith	219.411
30	Pancho Carter	212.998
74	Jim Crawford	210.482

had a lap at 219.411 and Pancho Carter turned a circuit at 212.996 for the day's best of that group.

Emerson Fittipaldi, in his #3T backup Marlboro Penske Mercedes, had the fastest lap of the day at 226.421 as the Penske team continued its vigorous testing program.

In all, only 18 cars were on the track, running just 603 laps.

Others found alternative things to do on a day that was largely "off," like chief starter Duane Sweeney.

Sweeney has made annual ventures for many years to area schools, speaking on the "500," his duties as starter and safety to youngsters. On this day, he attended a fifth-grade Career Day program at a school in Mooresville.

"The littlest ones want to become drivers," Sweeney said, "but many want to be a flagman. It's the best seat in the house."

But most track — and off-track — excursions would wait.

QUOTE OF THE DAY:
"I'm very proud of my dad's decision."
Al Unser, Jr.

TRACKSIDE FILES
DAY 11
TUESDAY, MAY 17

The on-track action took a back seat to the bombshells from the Trackside Conference Room on this day as Al Unser suddenly announced his retirement and Bobby Rahal said he and teammate Mike Groff had made alternative plans to make certain they stayed in the "500" field.

Unser, who only a few days earlier had renounced any intention of retirement, was first up in the conference room at 10:30 a.m., and choked back emotion as he closed the curtain on a career that took him to Victory Lane at Indianapolis on four separate occasions.

He had worked with the new Arizona Motor-Sport team, but had not gotten up to comfortable speed in practice.

"I've decided I'm not all there with the race car and I've decided to pull back and retire," Unser said. "If a driver doesn't produce 100 percent...I know the difference when I do not. I finally realized that I'm not doing what I should be doing. I always said when that day came, I'd back down. It's very sad. I'll tell you, it's hard."

Reactions to Unser's retirement were widespread. He had discussed the move with his son, Al Jr.

"I'm very proud of my dad's decision," Unser Jr. said. "I know it was very hard for him to make it. We talked about it and the Indianapolis 500 means a lot to my father. That's why it made it especially hard for him to decide this now."

"We were rookies together (in 1965)," said Mario Andretti, "teammates (Vel's Parnelli Jones Racing, 1972-75) and our sons have come along to enjoy their own careers. I can identify with his pride in Al Jr. winning the pole. In my book, Al Unser is one of the top five racers who has ever lived. Nobody had race savvy like Al in his prime."

Later in the day, Roberto Moreno, who had started the "500" in 1986 and finished 19th, took the seat in the Arizona entry and completed 10 laps of a 20-lap refresher.

Meanwhile, the Rahal-Hogan team was busy. It announced that it had acquired two 1993 Penske-Ilmor V8C cars as a contingency in the event Rahal and Groff were bumped on the final qualifying weekend.

Paul Tracy practiced one of the cars and ran 215.833. Rahal first practiced with the same car at 3:45 p.m., and less than two hours later, reached 222.833, his fastest practice speed of the month.

The backup Honda-powered cars went to the back burner as the Penske machines became the team's primary alternates.

"Our feeling is, we got everything we could get (from the Hondas)," Rahal said. "It's not enough at this point. We'll see what transpires this week with the possibility of bumping. However, we haven't seen the other backup cars yet and that caught us off guard last year. We'll play it as we go along and be ready to defend the position, no matter what."

Geoff Brabham was named as a driver for the Menard team's backup to Scott Brayton as backup plans started to become clear.

Mark Smith was the fastest of not-yet-qualified drivers at 219.947 in the #15 Craftsman Tool Ford. Jim Crawford was next at 217.003 in the #74 Riley & Scott entry. Four other drivers still seeking spots in the field were slower yet.

The search for speed was still on.

Date:	Tuesday, May 17
Weather:	Sunny, High 69°
Drivers On Track:	26
Cars On Track:	26
Total Laps:	1,005

Top Five Non-Qualified Drivers of the Day

Car	Driver	Speed
15	Mark Smith	219.947
74	Jim Crawford	217.003
40	Scott Goodyear	216.507
24	Willy T. Ribbs	215.750
30T	Pancho Carter	213.858

Top; A huge puff of smoke trailed behind Robby Gordon when his engine blew. Bottom; Bobby Rahal saddled-up his newly acquired Penske/Ilmor.

"It's very sad. I'll tell you, it's hard."
Al Unser

The second of only three drivers to have won the Indianapolis 500 four times, 1970, 1971, 1978 and 1987, Al Unser retires from competition having led more laps, 644, than any other driver in history. No less than 17 of his 27 starts between 1965 and 1993 resulted in placings within the top 12, while his trio of runnerup finishes, coupled with his four wins and four third-place showing represents an all-time record of 11 appearances within the top three. The 1970 pole sitter and a starter from the front two rows on 10 occasions, Al was the first person ever to drive against his own son in a "500." He also has the distinction of having a brother, Bobby, who has won the "500" three times as well as a son, Al Jr., who has won twice.

QUOTE OF THE DAY:
"I'd like to talk to him."
Mike Groff

TRACKSIDE FILES
DAY 12
WEDNESDAY, MAY 18

Jeff Andretti

It was a day of new deals, car-hopping and help.

Teams used different drivers in cars in an effort to build speed in the not-yet-qualified ranks, but Mark Smith's top lap of 220.324 in the #9 Valvoline Cummins Ford backup to Robby Gordon was the best of the rest.

Gordon and Smith each drove the car for Walker Racing as the team tried to work Smith into the field. Jeff Andretti was assigned to the #94 Hemelgarn Racing entry.

Mike Groff got his first ride in one of Rahal-Hogan's just-acquired Penske-Ilmor V8Cs. Scott Brayton and newly-named Menard driver Geoff Brabham each practiced in the car about to be assigned to the latter.

When the day concluded, Emerson Fittipaldi had continued as the busiest driver of the month, completing 676 laps in four different cars, followed by Teo Fabi with 649 laps in two cars. In all, 45 drivers had completed 16,504 laps at the Speedway during May. And it was getting closer

Date:	Wednesday, May 18
Weather:	Sunny, High 69°
Drivers On Track:	30
Cars On Track:	27
Total Laps:	1,480

Top Five Non-Qualified Drivers of the Day

Car	Driver	Speed
9	Mark Smith	220.324
46	John Paul, Jr.	218.643
30T	Pancho Carter	216.805
23	Buddy Lazier	216.357
40	Scott Goodyear	216.138

to the final two qualifying days to make the show. Groff was pleased with his first ride in the Penske machine.

"I'm not super comfortable in it but we'll work on it tonight," he said after scoring a lap at 221.560. "It's a great car. Roger (Penske) gave us a great opportunity and this car'll get it done. This car is very different, very unique. Paul (Tracy) shook it down. (Rick) Mears could give some good advice. I'd like to talk to him."

After Smith's 220-plus lap, seven other drivers not yet qualified had varying degrees of success in building speed.

John Paul Jr. was second fastest of this group at 218.643 in the #46 Pro Formance Racing Team Losi XX entry. Pancho Carter reached 216.805 in the #30T CYBERGENICS/Alfa Laval/Tetra Pak machine. Buddy Lazier got the #23 Financial World entry up to 216.357.

None, however, could be comfortable. More miles an hour would be needed within 72 hours, or many of these cars would be parked on Race Day.

Top; The pop-off valve caused a lot of discussion during the month. Above; Mike Groff had no problem adjusting to his new Penske/Ilmor.

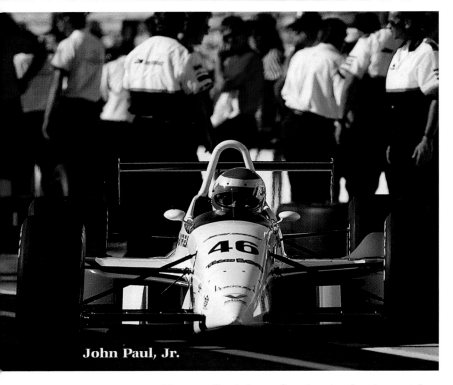

John Paul, Jr.

Gary Bettenhausen

The two final days of reckoning by time trials neared and teams were either turning up the effort to make the field, changing drivers, or dropping out of contention.

John Paul Jr., was the fastest not-yet-qualified driver of the day with a lap at 222.058 miles an hour in the #46 Pro Formance Team Losi XX machine. He was followed by Gary Bettenhausen in the #61 Bettenhausen Motorsports entry at 221.462 and Geoff Brabham, newly installed in the #59 Glidden Special, at 221.391.

Paul Jr. put in 19 laps in the car. He had waved off qualifying runs on both previous qualifying days in the 219-220 range.

"The car has speed there," he said. "We're confident we'll get it in the show. This is the third time and I'm not going to fail this time."

Davy Jones got his first laps in the #40T Budweiser King Special as the King Motorsports team started its move to get two cars in the show and a protection strategy for lead driver Scott Goodyear.

Date:	Thursday, May 19
Weather:	Cloudy, High 72°
Drivers On Track:	35
Cars On Track:	36
Total Laps:	1,005

Top Five Non-Qualified Drivers of the Day

Car	Driver	Speed
46	John Paul, Jr.	222.058
61	Gary Bettenhausen	221.462
59	Geoff Brabham	221.391
25	Marco Greco	220.108
23	Buddy Lazier	220.070

Tero Palmroth took over from Roberto Moreno in the #44 Arizona Motor-Sport Racing entry. Bryan Herta practiced the #41T A.J. Foyt Copenhagen Racing machine, a 1994 Lola/Ford, the car's first appearance of the month.

Meanwhile, others were finished. Dale Coyne said that his team would drop its pursuit of driver test completion for Ross Bentley. "The car he ran was not a competitive enough package to qualify," Coyne said.

And McCormack Motorsports dropped plans to get Fredrik Ekblom in the field. "We're waiting to get Pancho up (Carter) to speed," said Dennis McCormack. "Once we get him in the field, then we'll work with Fredrik."

Off track, other things were happening. Pole winner Al Unser Jr., was scheduled to throw up a ceremonial jump ball to start the Indiana Pacers-Atlanta Hawks NBA playoff game.

Herta and Paul Jr., with their teams, advanced to the quarterfinal round of the $51,000 Miller Genuine Draft Pit Crew Championship. Herta's Foyt crew posted a clocking of 12.990 seconds and Paul Jr.'s Pro Formance crew checked in at 13.420 seconds.

And Mario Illien, designer for Ilmor Engineering, was honored with the 28th annual Louis Schwitzer Award for the launching of the new Mercedes Benz engine that put Unser Jr. on the pole. Paul Ray, an Ilmor vice president, accepted the $5,000 check.

"The amount of effort that has gone into this has been crazy," Ray said. "Performance was there when we first put it on the dyno. Reliability was the issue all along. We think we've got the reliability side sorted out."

Ray's words were not exactly rays of hope for non-Penske teams for Race Day, although Ilmor first had an engine last 500 miles only on Day #2 of the month in a test at Michigan.

QUOTE OF THE DAY:
"I know I'm spreading myself too thin."
Dick Simon

TRACKSIDE FILES
DAY 14
FRIDAY, MAY 20

The final practice day of the month brought new faces to the track and also allowed some owners to talk about the month and the situations that faced them.

Jeff Sinden, co-owner of Arizona Motor-Sport Racing, had started the month with the now-retired Al Unser in the cockpit. Then came Roberto Moreno. Tero Palmroth had taken over for Moreno, but was officially named to drive the car on this day.

It was somewhat of a cooperative effort with Dick Simon Racing.

"I called Nelson (Piquet, after Unser retired) to see if he had any ideas and he mentioned Moreno to do some of the testing and help us go in the right direction," Sinden said. "Moreno was not coming here to race. Simon was wanting to do something with Palmroth but didn't have a car available. Simon's helped us and we've helped him through the years. Everybody's got good feelings."

Simon had his own reflections of the month. He had five cars in the field and was working with two others.

"I said last year I wouldn't run five cars again," he said. "I think 'won't that day ever come when we can concentrate on two or three cars?' But we have to do what we have to do. I know I'm spreading myself too thin. There's not as much time to fine-tune things as much as I'd like to."

Stephan Gregoire, the 1993 French rookie, made his first appearance of the month in a Simon machine, the #5T Duracell Charger

backup to Raul Boesel. Didier Theys was named to drive the #64 Project Indy Lola-Ford, a 1993 model which hadn't had a driver all month. His best lap was 206.820.

John Paul Jr. set the pace among the not-yet-qualified drivers for the third straight day with a lap at 221.691 in the #45 Pro Formance Team Losi XX machine., followed again by Gary Bettenhausen at 221.190 in the #61 Alumax Aluminum entry. They would be "first up" in the qualifying order the next day.

In all, 14 drivers with hopes to make the field took the track on the final preparation day, with Gregoire the slowest at 194.028.

There would be something else on the line... $80,000 in Speedway qualifying prizes, with $25,000 going to the fastest qualifier each day.

Alex Trotman, Ford Motor Company's chairman and chief executive officer, took his first laps ever at the Speedway to practice for the historic Race Day moment when he would join A.J. Foyt and Parnelli Jones in a three-car formation to lead the field through the parade laps.

"I enjoyed it," Trotman said after the three practiced in the Ford Mustang pace cars. "It was tremendous fun, just marvelous to be out here with A.J. and Parnelli. The cars felt great. We rehearsed exactly what we were going to do, did the formation stuff two or three times, then did the faster stuff."

He was asked about the thrill of heading the field.

"Nobody made a law against having some fun in your job and I'm taking advantage of that," he said.

Date:	Friday, May 20
Weather:	Cloudy, High 76°
Drivers On Track:	31
Cars On Track:	32
Total Laps:	1,154

Top Five Non-Qualified Drivers of the Day

Car	Driver	Speed
45	John Paul, Jr.	221.691
61	Gary Bettenhausen	221.190
40	Scott Goodyear	220.881
23	Buddy Lazier	219.609
59T	Geoff Brabham	219.288

Above left; Dick Simon was pleased with Stephan Gregoire's efforts in Raul Boesel's machine.
Above right; Gary Bettenhausen appeared to be going uphill from this unique perspective of the south short chute.
Bottom; Safely in the field, Robby Gordon sat back and enjoyed the view.

Bobby Rahal

Another retirement of a Speedway legend took place and strategy became fast and furious as some teams took chances and some played it safe on the third qualifying day.

At 10:45 a.m., three-time "500" winner Johnny Rutherford donned the helmet and gloves for the final time, climbed into a #14 AJ Foyt Copenhagen Racing car and made a final lap of honor before announcing his retirement as an active driver.

"Well, it's tough, really tough," Lone Star JR told spectators over the Speedway's public-address system. This was a really special thing for me. Thank you to all my fans and all my friends here at the Speedway. But it's time to say good bye to the cockpit. Now I know what A.J., Al Unser and Mario went through. Now, I'm the last of our gang to say "it's over." It's time to move over and make room. It was a thrill to be able to do this.

"I asked A.J., if I could go 222, could I put it at the end of the line," he added. "A.J. said, 'go ahead.'"

With the recent retirements of Foyt, Unser, Andretti (at the end of the season), Rutherford and Rick Mears, the winners of 16 Indianapolis 500s had, as JR put it, "made room." The guard was changing.

Another veteran also stepped back for the weekend. Pancho Carter was released from his commitment to drive for McCormack Motorsports.

"This morning, Pancho called to tell me that he felt that he could not give us 100 percent and no longer wanted to drive our race car," said team owner Dennis McCormack.

Gary Bettenhausen, who started his career just a few short years after Rutherford, saw his month of May hopes go into the inside wall off the second turn. The car sustained heavy right rear damage, but Bettenhausen was examined and cleared to drive.

"The car got loose and spun," he said. "It spun so fast I couldn't save it. It knocked the rear end off. What will be, will be."

As scheduled, John Paul Jr., was first up for qualifying and completed a crisp run in the #45 Pro Formance Team Losi XX Lola at 222.500.

Paul Jr.'s qualifying run touched off a wacky time trial day in which seven qualifiers filled three open spots in the field with only one car being bumped.

Rookie Marco Greco was next, but waved off after three laps in the #25T Arciero Project Indy entry.

Then came Scott Goodyear, who had had problems all month, and he checked in at a chancy 220.737 in the #40 Budweiser King Special.

Goodyear's run came just 12 minutes after Paul Jr.'s. The track temperature was 113 degrees when qualifying began. Others would wait for the "happy hour" rush.

During the ensuing practice, Roberto Guerrero's #21T Interstate Batteries/Pagan Racing machine had an engine fire and Guerrero slid it down to the turn #4 grass. He suffered minor first and second degree burns and was cleared to drive.

But strategy was building.

When the rush came, Mauricio Gugelmin's #89 Hollywood Indy Car was pushed into line. He had qualified the previous weekend, but the Chip Ganassi team elected to withdraw the qualified car and take the chance that Gugelmin would be safer with the backup.

Gugelmin didn't disappoint them, checking in at a four-lap average of 223.104 miles an hour, much faster — and safer — than the 220.460 recorded a week earlier.

Mark Smith, after a frustrating month, then qualified the #15 Craftsman Tool Ford at 220.683 at 5:37 p.m.

When Davy Jones went out to qualify the #40T Budweiser King Special, more strategy evolved.

Above; Driving for brother Tony (left), Gary Bettenhausen missed the show as a result of a crash in turn #2. Left; Emerson Fittipaldi received an honorary baton from the Green Berets during the Armed Forces Day presentations.

35

Davy Jones

Buddy Lazier

Jones was in a "protection" position for the King Motorsports team to try to put the car in the show in case it was needed by Goodyear getting into a bumped position. Also, if King could get two cars in, so be it.

While Jones was on his qualifying run of 223.817 miles an hour, plenty healthy to make the show, the qualified #10T of Mike Groff was withdrawn. Groff was first on the bump list and teammate Bobby Rahal was second.

Groff was next in line, followed by Rahal in the Rahal-Hogan team's newly acquired Penske-Ilmors. As Jones was clearly making the field, Rahal-Hogan assistant team manager Scott Roembke worked the rules and the clock in making the calls.

Out went Groff at 5:46 p.m., and he smoothly took the #52T Motorola Penske to an average of 221.355. During his run, Rahal's already qualified Honda-powered machine was withdrawn.

Next came Rahal at 5:51 p.m., and he put the #50 Miller Genuine Draft Penske into the show at 224.094, the fastest qualifier of the day, to bump Smith from the field.

"This place takes a lot of strategy," said Carl Hogan, co-owner of the Groff and Rahal efforts. "I think Scott knew the rules exactly and he played it perfectly."

"Mike was going to be the first bump, so we had to get him to respond first," Rahal said. "We didn't think Davy Jones was going to have the run he had and Mark Smith...that's the fastest he's gone all month. I'm so pleased this ordeal is over. There were some hard choices to make."

Tero Palmroth and Buddy Lazier took aborted runs, but the field was full and one final day awaited.

Date:	Saturday, May 21	
Weather:	Sunny, High 82°	
Qualification Attempts:	10	
Qualifiers:	7	

Today's Qualifiers

Car	Driver	Speed
50	Bobby Rahal	224.094
	(Bumps #15 Smith)	
40T	Davy Jones	223.817
89	Mauricio Gugelmin	223.104
45	John Paul, Jr.	222.500
52T	Mike Groff	221.355
40	Scott Goodyear	220.737
	(Bumped by #25T Greco)	
15	Mark Smith	220.683
	(Bumped by #50 Rahal)	

"It's time to say goodbye to the cockpit."
Johnny Rutherford

Three times the victor of the Indianapolis 500 and three times the pole winner, Johnny Rutherford came within one-fifth of a second of turning the first-ever 200 mph lap when he recorded 199.071 mph during qualifications in 1973. He was participating in the "500" for the 11th time when he won in 1974 and, had it not been for a rainstorm terminating the 1975 event with 25 laps to go while he was catching Bobby Unser, he might have recorded consecutive triumphs. He returned to the winner's circle in 1976, thus having placed either first or second in three straight years. He added a third victory in 1980. He participated in a total of 24 "500s," starting from the front row four times, placing in the top ten eight times and leading for 196 laps.

Mark Smith failed to make the field for the second year in a row after hitting the wall late in the day.

Willy T. Ribbs

The agony of waiting set in as track temperatures reached 119 degrees when qualifying was scheduled to open.

None of the remaining teams figured it could overcome the loss of a few precious miles an hour by running in the heat, leaving their efforts to last-ditch banzai attempts late in the day.

Scott Goodyear was on the bubble at 220.737 miles an hour, the fastest speed ever for a slowest qualifier in an Indianapolis 500 field.

It would be a formidable task for those remaining to knock Goodyear out of the "500", but the Bettenhausen Motorsports team miraculously repaired Gary Bettenhausen's damaged machine overnight.

The team took an underwing off a spare car and put in a new gearbox, working until 3 a.m. to give the veteran driver another shot to get in the show.

In the morning practice, only Geoff Brabham in the #59T Glidden Special had reached a speed capable of bumping Goodyear, with one lap at

221.359. Robby Gordon, in a not-yet-qualified #9 Valvoline Cummins Ford, reached 222.916, leaving railbirds to speculate whether Walker Racing teammates Willy T. Ribbs or Mark Smith would wind up in the seat at "happy hour."

Stephan Gregoire practiced the #30 CYBER-GENICS/Alfa Laval Tetra Pak entry. Buddy Lazier practiced the #5T Duracell Charger from the Simon stable. By mid-afternoon, the Riley & Scott team and driver Jim Crawford called it quits for the month.

The rush to the line occurred at 5:30 p.m., when Marco Greco and the #25T Arciero Project Indy machine was pushed in line, closely followed by everyone else who wanted to try. The track temperature was 107 degrees. It would not be easy.

But Greco reeled off a smooth run of 221.216 miles an hour to bump Goodyear from the field, touching off a wild half hour with Bryan Herta's AJ Foyt machine on the bubble.

"It was really tough to just watch all day," Greco said. "That was the toughest part, but I was so

happy to be here. I told the crew, 'don't talk to me until I finish.'"

Brabham was next up in the #59T Glidden Special, but waved off after his speeds dropped from 221.190 to 219.990 in three laps.

Smith was next, in the #15T Craftsman Tool Ford. But he brushed the right side of the car against the wall in Turn #1, slid through the south short chute and hit the wall again with the left side. When he started his run, only 15 minutes remained. Smith was checked at the Hanna Medical Center and cleared to drive, but Ribbs jumped into the Walker team's spare #9 car originally assigned to Gordon.

When the accident debris was cleared, Bettenhausen ran two laps in the 218 bracket in the repaired Bettenhausen Motorsports car and waved off.

Ribbs was last to go, with just a minute remaining. But his two laps were 216.206 and 212.942, well too slow.

"It was a long shot," Ribbs said. "The car was nice, but I was unfamiliar with it. We had every-

Willy T. Ribbs had his father's moral support during his efforts to make the show.

39

thing to gain and nothing to lose. You go out with no negative thoughts in mind — just positives. The last two times I was here was the greatest part of my life."

For Herta, it was the end of a nail-biter. The Foyt team had the #41T backup car in line and Herta had practiced in it at more than 223 miles an hour. But the team elected to pull the backup out of line and take its chances.

"I thought he had a lot of respect for me when I asked him (Herta) to make the call (on whether to pull the car out of line)," said Foyt. "He said, 'no, you make the call.' I said okay, let's pull it out and he said, 'okay.'"

Qualifying for the 78th Indianapolis 500 was over.

Above; A member of the safety crew relaxed during a lull in the action. Right; The Naval guard proudly presented the colors. Bottom; A.J. Foyt and rookie Bryan Herta made the right decision not to requalify.

	Date:	Sunday, May 22
	Weather:	Sunny, High 89°
Qualification Attempts:	5	
Qualifiers:	1	

Today's Qualifiers

Car	Driver	Speed
25T	Marco Greco (Bumps #40 Goodyear)	221.216

QUOTE OF THE DAY:
"If you see the blimp, duck."
Robby Gordon

TRACKSIDE FILES
DAY 17
THURSDAY, MAY 26

Left; Marlboro was one of many sponsors to participate in the Indy 500 Expo. Bottom; IMS President Tony George (front right) and Gary Grahn, Jr. tested their mechanical skills during a pit stop contest at the Indy 500 Expo.

It was only fitting on the final Carburetion Day of his career that Mario Andretti was the fastest.

Andretti posted a quickest speed of 223.708 in 19 laps of practice to be fastest of the day, followed by Scott Brayton at 222.905 and Emerson Fittipaldi at 222.872.

A total of 34 cars — the starting field plus alternate Mark Smith, took the track. Arie Luyendyk ran the most laps with 28. Lyn St. James ran the least, with six.

"The car is capable," Andretti said. "That's the important thing. We're going to leave it alone until Race Day. We moved over the setup from the other car to achieve the balance and hope it's inside the envelope for Sunday. The car felt fine testing it out in the traffic today."

Off the track, railbirds had watched the moves all week of the King Motorsports team, which reversed itself several times in trying to create the best possible situation for both of its drivers, Scott Goodyear and Davy Jones, to make the show.

The team had announced that Goodyear would drive its one qualified car after switching with Davy Jones, putting Jones in the first alternate car. But it would make its official request after Carburetion Day.

41

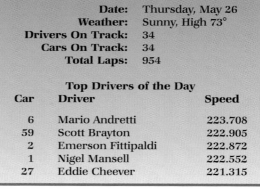

Mario Andretti

Top; The Forsythe-Green crew clocked the fastest pit stop to win the Miller Genuine Draft Pit Crew Championship. Bottom; The 33 starters plus first alternate Davy Jones paraded through pit lane during the last practice session.

The finals of the $51,000 Miller Genuine Draft Pit Crew Championships were held and the Forsythe-Green crew, led by crew chief Kyle Moyer, of Jacques Villeneuve captured the 18th annual event with a time of 12.867 seconds, the second-fastest time in contest history.

The Forsythe-Green crew beat the crew of John Paul Jr.'s Pro Formance Racing entry, which posted a clocking of 13.590 seconds. The Pro Formance crew had to advance through the quarterfinals and beat Al Unser Jr.'s Penske crew in the semifinals.

"I think he (Villeneuve) is a bit surprised on how we did, but the team's been working really hard to get here," Moyer said after the Forsythe-Green team beat Raul Boesel's Dick Simon crew in the semifinals.

But the focus of attention was the Penske team and preparations for dealing with it on Race Day.

Some, like Robby Gordon, planned diversions.

"Tonight at 5 o'clock, I'm flying the Goodyear blimp," Gordon said. "I'm going to try to fly low under the radar. If you see the blimp, duck."

Rookie Dennis Vitolo had been "adopted" the previous day by a kindergarten class in Fall Creek. Vitolo had visited the class, took a helmet and driver's suit and talked to the youngsters about safety.

The class drew some racing pictures for him and they were put on display in the Dick Simon garage. Vitolo's favorite was a picture upon which was written, "My car goes 100 miles an hour, no I mean a trillion. It goes a trillion fast. It's made of metal and nothing can break it. Signed, Jacob."

Vitolo mused, "sounds like a Penske car."

Date:	Thursday, May 26
Weather:	Sunny, High 73°
Drivers On Track:	34
Cars On Track:	34
Total Laps:	954

Top Drivers of the Day

Car	Driver	Speed
6	Mario Andretti	223.708
59	Scott Brayton	222.905
2	Emerson Fittipaldi	222.872
1	Nigel Mansell	222.552
27	Eddie Cheever	221.315

> **"I sure thought I would have a chance to win more than one."**
> *Mario Andretti*

In view of his phenomenal rate of success in what has unquestionably been the most extraordinarily diversified career in motorsports history, it is inconceivable that Mario Andretti was never able to repeat his Indianapolis 500 triumph of 1969. He qualified either for the first or second row in an amazing 20 out of his 29 starts and yet he only survived to the checkered flag in nine of them. He led for 556 laps in "500" competition, third only to Al Unser and Ralph DePalma, and he is the only driver in history to have led the greatest number of laps in a "500" four times. He is also the only driver ever to have led the greatest number of laps in what turned out to be a non-winning effort three times. Competitive to the very end, Mario was running fourth when forced out of his final Indianapolis 500 in 1994.

43

500

Winner's Circle
Honor Roll Student
Kelly Glover

FESTIVAL

North St

31

500 Festival Queen
Jennifer Lyn Swanson

DRIVERS TEST

Oscar Mayer

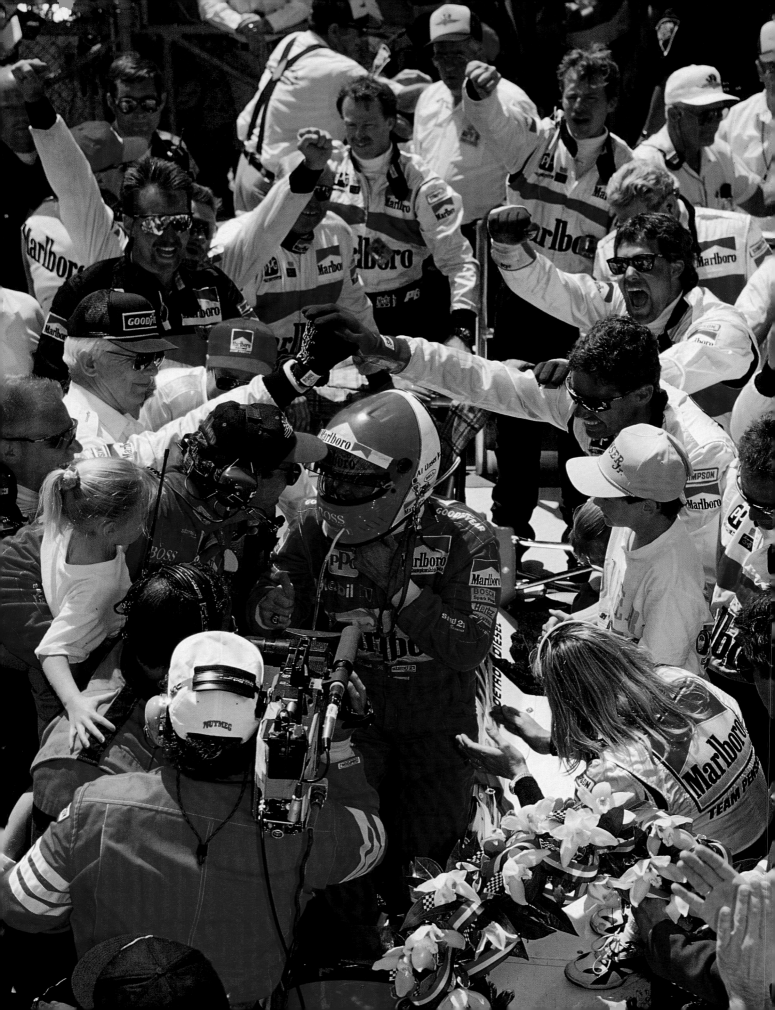

WINNER
AL UNSER, JR.

#31 Marlboro Penske Mercedes
Entrant: Penske Racing, Inc.   Crew Chief: Richard Buck

1994 PENSKE/MERCEDES BENZ

Starting Position:	1
Qualifying Average:	228.011 MPH
Qualifying Speed Rank:	1
Best Practice Speed:	229.481 MPH 5/14
Total Practice Laps:	707
Number Practice Days:	12
Finishing Position:	1
Laps Completed:	200 160.872 MPH
Highest Position 1994 Race:	1
Fastest Race Lap:	12 217.986 MPH
1994 Prize Money:	$1,373,813
INDY 500 Career Earnings:	$4,262,690
Career INDY 500 Starts:	12
Career Best Finish:	1st 1992, 1994

Al Unser, Jr. started his month at Michigan International Speedway, where Penske's test team was putting the finishing touches on the new Mercedes Benz engine.

Unser Jr. didn't get on the track at Indy until Day #3 and wasted no time cracking into the top 10, getting eighth at 223.897 miles an hour. He topped the speed chart on Day #5 at 226.478 and had his fastest lap of the month at 227.618 in the morning practice before the first qualifying session. Unser Jr. registered a four-lap average of 228.011, best at the time.

"I got caught in the rain this morning during practice going for 229 and I almost crashed," Unser Jr. said. "During the qualifying run, when I saw the 225,

I thought, 'Oh man, I need to go after it.' And I did. It was like looking down a double-barreled shotgun staring at ya', but each lap got quicker and quicker. It was just great."

The final try at the pole on Sunday was by his teammate, Fittipaldi, who wound up third fastest and Unser Jr., together with his father, became the first son and father to have ever won a pole at Indy.

On Race Day, Unser Jr. dueled Fittipaldi. In all, Unser Jr. led 48 laps, taking the lead for good on lap #185 when Fittipaldi crashed while trying to lap Unser Jr. So Unser Jr. got his second Indianapolis 500 victory during a month of May in which his father, a three-time winner, retired.

2nd PLACE
JACQUES VILLENEUVE

#12 Player's LTD Forsythe-Green

1994 Reynard Ford

Entrant: Forsythe/Green Racing, Inc.   **Crew Chief:** Kyle Moyer

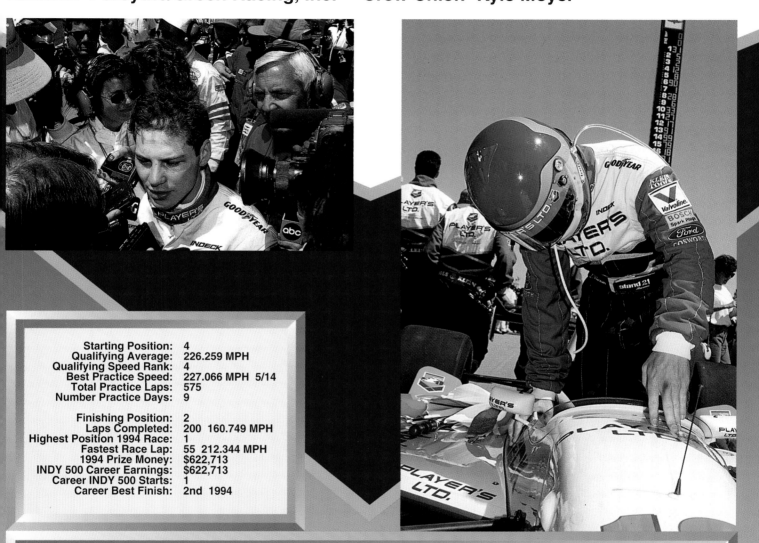

Starting Position:	4
Qualifying Average:	226.259 MPH
Qualifying Speed Rank:	4
Best Practice Speed:	227.066 MPH 5/14
Total Practice Laps:	575
Number Practice Days:	9
Finishing Position:	2
Laps Completed:	200 160.749 MPH
Highest Position 1994 Race:	1
Fastest Race Lap:	55 212.344 MPH
1994 Prize Money:	$622,713
INDY 500 Career Earnings:	$622,713
Career INDY 500 Starts:	1
Career Best Finish:	2nd 1994

Jacques Villeneuve started the month as one of Indy's most promising rookies. He passed the observation phase of his driver's test on the first day and cracked the top 10 on the speed chart on the next day with a lap at 222.651.

He recorded his fastest lap of the month the morning before the first qualifying session at 227.066, fifth fastest of the final practice.

He reeled off a smooth four-lap run of 226.259 to start fourth. Both his average and his one-lap best of 227.061 were records for rookie drivers at Indy.

"I did not expect to be this fast," Villeneuve said. "The last two laps were slower because I had to bring it down in the corners. It's just great to be here."

When the green flag dropped, he quickly fell to eighth and out of the top 10 by the 100-mile mark.

But he stormed back. He was third at 150 miles and in all, he took the lead twice for a total of seven laps and became the race's only leader other than Al Unser Jr. and Fittipaldi.

When Fittipaldi crashed, it left Villeneuve in second behind Al Unser Jr. and he finished only 8.6 seconds behind the winner in his first "500" start.

"It feels fantastic," Villeneuve said. "Before coming here, I never dreamed of being on the podium. Actually, I was hoping to but I never was thinking I could make it."

3rd PLACE
BOBBY RAHAL

1993 PENSKE/ILMOR

#4 Miller Genuine Draft
Entrant: Rahal/Hogan Racing   **Crew Chief:** Larry Ellert

Starting Position:	28
Qualifying Average:	224.094 MPH
Qualifying Speed Rank:	7
Best Practice Speed:	226.102 MPH 5/21
Total Practice Laps:	646
Number Practice Days:	13
Finishing Position:	3
Laps Completed:	199 Running
Highest Position 1994 Race:	3
Fastest Race Lap:	195 216.664 MPH
1994 Prize Money:	$411,163
INDY 500 Career Earnings:	$2,416,329
Career INDY 500 Starts:	12
Career Best Finish:	1st 1986

Bobby Rahal and the Rahal-Hogan team worked to develop the new Honda engine and when Pole Day arrived, he qualified at only 220.178.

"It is certainly not by design, I tell you," Rahal said. "I was flat out on four laps with the best speeds we ran. I would have liked to run a little quicker, but you can only put it down so far. I was pretty pleased. This was the first time the car did the same thing for all four laps."

The speed was ominously slow, so the team hedged its bets, acquiring a pair of 1993 Penskes with Ilmor powerplants as a cushion.

"We'll see what transpires this week with the possibility of bumping," Rahal said. "We haven't seen other backup cars yet, and that caught us off guard last year. We'll play it as we go along and be ready to defend the position, no matter what."

On the third qualifying day, Groff took out the first Penske, Rahal's qualified car was withdrawn, and he was in line with the other. He put together a run of 224.094, safely in the show.

On Race Day, Rahal started 28th, moving steadily to fourth at 200 miles and stayed in the top 10 throughout the day. At the end, his three fastest laps came on the 193rd, 194th and 195th circuits and they were among the 50 fastest of the day as he charged to a third-place finish.

4th PLACE
JIMMY VASSER

#18 Conseco-STP
Entrant: Hayhoe Racing, Inc.   Crew Chief: Phil Casey

1994 REYNARD FORD

Starting Position:	16
Qualifying Average:	222.262 MPH
Qualifying Speed Rank:	24
Best Practice Speed:	226.803 MPH 5/13
Total Practice Laps:	465
Number Practice Days:	13
Finishing Position:	4
Laps Completed:	199 Running
Highest Position 1994 Race:	3
Fastest Race Lap:	117 211.750 MPH
1994 Prize Money:	$295,163
INDY 500 Career Earnings:	$654,019
Career INDY 500 Starts:	3
Career Best Finish:	4th 1994

Jimmy Vasser started the month at a fast pace, cracking the top 10 in practice on Day #5 with a lap at 223.303 miles an hour. The day before Pole Day he was still in the hunt, with a lap at 226.803.

He had to watch on Pole Day as Hideshi Matsuda, broke his four-lap rookie record of 222.313 miles an hour set in 1992. When the day ended, he was one of those left in line to go on Sunday. He went out at 1:13 p.m. and registered a four-lap run of 222.262, becoming the 24th qualifier.

"It's a bit of a relief to get to qualify after sitting around all day yesterday and some today," Vasser said.

On Race Day, he started 16th but he charged to the front quickly, jumping into eighth place by the 75-mile mark. At 150 miles, he was fourth on the lead lap, trailing only Fittipaldi, Unser Jr. and Villeneuve, then moved to third on lap #62.

Although he dropped back during the race's middle stages, he was back to fourth at 300 miles and wound up in that spot, just one lap down.

"It feels pretty darned good," Vasser said of his best-ever "500" finish. "Race conditions were not that bad, even though there was a lot of turbulence out there. The Indy 500 is the biggest race. We can really build on this race...not just this one, but every one counts."

5th PLACE
ROBBY GORDON

#9 Valvoline Cummins Ford
Entrant: Walker Racing   Crew Chief: Dan Miller

1994 LOLA/FORD

Starting Position:	19
Qualifying Average:	221.293 MPH
Qualifying Speed Rank:	29
Best Practice Speed:	227.739 MPH 5/14
Total Practice Laps:	662
Number Practice Days:	11
Finishing Position:	5
Laps Completed:	199 Running
Highest Position 1994 Race:	3
Fastest Race Lap:	157 212.791 MPH
1994 Prize Money:	$227,563
INDY 500 Career Earnings:	$383,016
Career INDY 500 Starts:	2
Career Best Finish:	5th 1994

Robby Gordon started the month of May on a mission as the lead driver for Walker Racing.

He jumped into the top 10 on Day #6, sixth fastest at 226.946. He was fourth fastest in the final practice before qualifying at 227.739, his fastest lap of the month.

He waved off while making the 10th qualifying run of the day after laps at 222-plus and 220-plus. The next day, in his backup car, he settled for a four-lap average of 221.293.

"I'm disappointed," Gordon said. "I know the heat was a factor and I'm not happy with 221. One lap we ran 227 in the #9 car and the next time around the lap meter blew up. There's a big difference.

Yesterday, the high was 62 degrees and it's already at 78 degrees today. The track changes, as you know."

On Race Day, after starting 19th, Gordon, reached third place by lap #64 and being in the hunt. He remained steadily in the top 10 until rolling to a fifth-place finish at the end, one lap off the pace. An early pit stop set him back.

"We had a bad set of tires," Gordon said. "The car was so loose, so loose it scared me. We got real loose toward the end of fuel every time. We tried to dial it in, but could never quite find it. I'm very happy. The team did a great job all day. This race team can win some races here. We just missed the boat a little bit."

1994 REYNARD/FORD

6th PLACE
MICHAEL ANDRETTI

#8 Target/Scotch Video Chip Ganassi Racing
Entrant: Chip Ganassi Racing Teams   Crew Chief: Mike Hull

Starting Position:	5
Qualifying Average:	226.205 MPH
Qualifying Speed Rank:	5
Best Practice Speed:	228.600 MPH 5/14
Total Practice Laps:	545
Number Practice Days:	11
Finishing Position:	6
Laps Completed:	198 Running
Highest Position 1994 Race:	2
Fastest Race Lap:	11 216.794 MPH
1994 Prize Money:	$245,563
INDY 500 Career Earnings:	$2,095,868
Career INDY 500 Starts:	10
Career Best Finish:	2nd 1991

Michael Andretti returned to Indy after a year's absence with a new chassis - the Reynard - and Chip Ganassi Racing for the first time.

He didn't waste a lot of time putting up numbers, reaching the top of the speed chart for Day #3 at 227.038 and staying among the frontrunners throughout the first week of practice.

He was third fastest in the morning practice before Pole Day qualifying with a lap at 228.600, trailing only Nigel Mansell and his father, Mario.

His time-trial run, the sixth of the day, averaged 226.205 and his front row stay lasted well into the qualifying line before being nudged back to fifth.

"I'm very happy to be back in Indy," Michael said. "It feels good. Chip Ganassi and the Target team came together nicely."

On Race Day, he jumped two spots to third on the first lap and chased Emerson Fittipaldi and Al Unser Jr. throughout the early going. He moved to second on lap #26 before settling for sixth at the finish.

"The thing that killed us was a cut tire after a long yellow...lap #29," Michael said. "When it went green, I almost lost the car in turn #4 and when I got to turn #1, I knew I had a flat tire. After I made that pit stop, it got us out of sync and caused us to lose a lap."

7th PLACE
TEO FABI

#11 Pennzoil Special
Entrant: Hall Racing, Inc.   Crew Chief: Alexander Hering

1994 REYNARD/ILMOR

Starting Position:	24
Qualifying Average:	223.394 MPH
Qualifying Speed Rank:	13
Best Practice Speed:	226.855 MPH 5/14
Total Practice Laps:	729
Number Practice Days:	12
Finishing Position:	7
Laps Completed:	198 Running
Highest Position 1994 Race:	7
Fastest Race Lap:	115 210.743 MPH
1994 Prize Money:	$216,563
INDY 500 Career Earnings:	$951,114
Career INDY 500 Starts:	7
Career Best Finish:	7th 1994

Teo Fabi was fast out of the gate, turning a lap at 223.703 miles an hour to be seventh quickest on the first day of practice.

Although he didn't crack the daily top 10 again, he recorded the fifth fastest speed, 226.855, in the morning practice before the first qualifying session. When his turn came, he waved off after one lap at just below 221 miles an hour. Later that day, in a backup car, he waved off again after two slow laps.

From there, he returned to his primary mount, and with just more than an hour remaining on the second day, put it in the show with a four-lap average of 223.394. He wound up starting 24th.

"It was a good run," Fabi said. "I had trouble with my popoff valve. I'm not blaming the valve — it's just that we need to learn to work with it. The car could have gone faster but it doesn't pay off to take a risk since I have to start so far back on the grid, anyway.

"Yesterday...I was convinced I could do 227 during qualifying. During qualifying, my first lap was 220 and my second lap was 222. During both laps, my valve wouldn't close. I finally managed to lose it at the end of the second lap when Jim Hall waved me in. It was a very difficult day."

On Race Day, Fabi charged through the pack, reaching 10th at 300 miles. He jumped two positions to seventh, where he stayed, two laps down at the finish.

1993 LOLA/MENARD

#27 Quaker State Special
Crew Chief: Tim Broyles

Entrant: Team Menard, Inc.

Starting Position:	11
Qualifying Average:	223.163 MPH
Qualifying Speed Rank:	15
Best Practice Speed:	228.676 MPH 5/10
Total Practice Laps:	554
Number Practice Days:	11
Finishing Position:	8
Laps Completed:	197 Running
Highest Position 1994 Race:	3
Fastest Race Lap:	190 214.597 MPH
1994 Prize Money:	$238,563
INDY 500 Career Earnings:	$1,002,446
Career INDY 500 Starts:	5
Career Best Finish:	4th 1992

Eddie Cheever returned to the Menard team for a second year.

He was third fastest on the first full day of practice with a lap at 223.998 miles an hour and stayed in the top 10 through much of the first week.

He hit 228.676 early in the week and posted a lap at 227.106 in the morning session before Pole Day qualifying. He was second out when time trials opened and his average was slower at 223.163 for the four laps.

"I'm disappointed," Cheever said. "The whole week we've been plagued with the popoff valve. It's kind of been a chain around my neck. I'm going to seriously consider bringing out the 'T' car. We had lots of problems trying to regulate our boost. It was kind of a roll of the dice to go out and try to get the right setup."

He started 11th in the field and ran as high as third on lap #42. He hovered in the top 10 until settling for eighth at the finish, three laps down despite a stop-and-go penalty.

"The car ran really well," Cheever said. "It's a pity I got that stop-and-go penalty. I don't know what that was all about. The USAC official made the decision. If he's right, okay, it was a good decision but I have to find out. It took us out of the race."

9th PLACE
BRYAN HERTA

#14 A.J. Foyt Copenhagen Racing
Entrant: A.J. Foyt Enterprises   Crew Chief: Craig Baranouski

1994 LOLA/FORD

Starting Position:	22
Qualifying Average:	220.992 MPH
Qualifying Speed Rank:	33
Best Practice Speed:	223.947 MPH 5/14
Total Practice Laps:	587
Number Practice Days:	10
Finishing Position:	9
Laps Completed:	197 Running
Highest Position 1994 Race:	8
Fastest Race Lap:	121 210.832 MPH
1994 Prize Money:	$212,213
INDY 500 Career Earnings:	$212,213
Career INDY 500 Starts:	1
Career Best Finish:	9th 1994

Bryan Herta started out the month of May as a rookie with a dream, entered originally in a car by Tasman Motorsports.

But his aspirations changed, as he posted the fastest practice laps of USAC's Rookie Orientation Program at 218-plus in a car fielded by the legendary A.J. Foyt.

When he made his run at 5:36 p.m. on Pole Day, he registered a speed of 220.992.

"I'm so happy to be in the show," he said. "I felt we had a good race car. That takes the butterflies out. We'll be in good shape for the race."

As qualifying wound down, Herta found himself on the bubble, and he and Foyt had to make a decision on whether to stay in line with a backup car or stand their ground with the qualified one.

"I thought he had a lot of respect for me when I asked him to make the call (on whether to pull the #41T out of line)," Foyt said. "He said, 'no, you make the call.' I said okay, let's pull out and he said okay."

And Herta had made his first "500" field.

On Race Day, he was steady, rolling to ninth at the finish, just three laps off the pace.

"I loved it," Herta said. "I really enjoyed racing here. I thought it'd be a lot tougher to pass than it was. When A.J. came on the radio and said, 'halfway,' I thought, 'man, just halfway?' I thought it was almost over."

1994 LOLA/FORD

#33 A.J. Foyt/Jonathan Byrd's Cafeteria/Bryant
Entrant: Jonathan Byrd/A.J. Foyt Racing   Crew Chief: Timothy Bumps

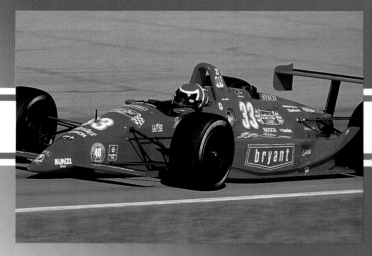

Starting Position:	10
Qualifying Average:	223.263 MPH
Qualifying Speed Rank:	14
Best Practice Speed:	224.310 MPH 5/14
Total Practice Laps:	228
Number Practice Days:	8
Finishing Position:	10
Laps Completed:	196 Running
Highest Position 1994 Race:	3
Fastest Race Lap:	42 210.773 MPH
1994 Prize Money:	$191,750
INDY 500 Career Earnings:	$1,140,935
Career INDY 500 Starts:	7
Career Best Finish:	5th 1991

John Andretti had a ride from the month's start in a car fielded by Jonathan Byrd and A.J. Foyt.

On Wednesday, Day #5 of the month, he got his Indy machine up to 221.544 miles an hour, eighth fastest of the day.

On Pole Day, he was the 15th qualifier at an average speed of 223.263, good enough for 10th starting spot.

"The weather is helping, obviously," Andretti said. "We hadn't quite hit the right combination yet. A.J. and the guys came up with some new things. They let Bryan (Herta, his teammate) try it. Bryan guaranteed me I'd like it. We were hoping the weather would cooperate and it did, somewhat."

On Race Day, he was sixth at 75 miles, fifth at 100 miles and third at 125 miles before settling back. He cracked back into the hunt to finish 10th, four laps down.

"At the beginning, we got to third but we just couldn't keep the balance in the car," Andretti said. "The car got real loose as the day went on. The guys worked real hard. I'm not satisfied. Tenth just means you're the ninth loser. I mean, seven years at Indy...you have to finish on top here. I felt like we had a real good shot at winning."

11th PLACE
MAURICIO GUGELMIN

#88 Hollywood Indy Car Chip Ganassi Racing

1994 REYNARD/FORD

Entrant: Chip Ganassi Racing Teams   Crew Chief: Grant Weaver

Starting Position:	29
Qualifying Average:	223.104 MPH
Qualifying Speed Rank:	16
Best Practice Speed:	226.182 MPH 5/21
Total Practice Laps:	457
Number Practice Days:	11
Finishing Position:	11
Laps Completed:	196 Running
Highest Position 1994 Race:	11
Fastest Race Lap:	140 208.411 MPH
1994 Prize Money:	$169,500
INDY 500 Career Earnings:	$169,500
Career INDY 500 Starts:	1
Career Best Finish:	11th 1994

Mauricio Gugelmin came to Indy as teammate to Michael Andretti for Chip Ganassi Racing.

On Day #5, he had cracked the top 10 in practice with a lap at 221.288 and pole qualifying awaited.

As the qualifying line wove its way around rain, Gugelmin went out 15 minutes from the close of first-day time trials and recorded a four-lap run of 220.460 to become the month's 19th qualifier.

"I don't know if I'll be in the race," Gugelmin said. "People went a lot faster than people anticipated. I ran a good first lap but then the car started to push and it was very disappointing."

When time trials started on the third day, the team elected to withdraw the qualified car to try to get more speed from the backup.

The strategy worked, as Gugelmin put together a four-lap run of 223.104 to safely get into the field.

"This morning I ran 226," he said. "We made a decision today. It was a gamble. I always felt comfortable with this car. Pulling the other car was a risk. We felt this was a better setup. It's a weight coming off your shoulders."

From a 29th-place start, Gugelmin ran fast and steadily to an 11th-place finish.

"Basically, we learned a lot," he said. "I'm glad we finished. I learned a lot and I'm pretty sure next year we're going to be a lot better."

1993 LOLA/FORD

#19 The Mi-Jack Car

Entrant: Dale Coyne Racing　**Crew Chief: Bernie Myers**

Starting Position:	21
Qualifying Average:	221.107 MPH
Qualifying Speed Rank:	32
Best Practice Speed:	228.519 MPH 5/14
Total Practice Laps:	686
Number Practice Days:	10
Finishing Position:	12
Laps Completed:	194 Running
Highest Position 1994 Race:	12
Fastest Race Lap:	63 207.823 MPH
1994 Prize Money:	$180,763
INDY 500 Career Earnings:	$180,763
Career INDY 500 Starts:	1
Career Best Finish:	12 1994

Brian Till's task was to spur a better month of May for Dale Coyne Racing, which had had a tough year in '93.

He built up to speed during the first week, and recorded his fastest practice lap the morning of Pole Day with a speed of 223.519. As rain played a role in qualifying, Till rolled out at 5:24 p.m. on Pole Day and registered a four-lap average of 221.107.

"I could get bumped, but it was a pretty good speed," Till said. "It was very nerve-wracking. All you can do is go out there and do the best you can. Our bottom line was 220 and I was a little disappointed watching (Bryan) Herta and (Mauricio) Gugelmin. I had my foot down 99 percent of the time but I thought it would be higher."

On Race Day, he started 21st but drove a steady trouble-free race to 12th, six laps down.

"We did what we set out to do — finish in the points," Till said. "After everything Dale (Coyne, the car owner) and his team went through last year, I'm glad we were able to bring the car home intact.

"The start was something you really have to experience to describe," he added. "I also learned a lot about how the track changes as the race progresses. I'm proud to be a part of the class of '94 here and I'm happy to say that I'm not a rookie here any more."

13th PLACE
STAN FOX

#91 Delta Faucet-Jack's Tool Rental-Hemelgarn Racing
Entrant: Hemelgarn Racing, Inc.   Crew Chief: Dan Basala

1994 REYNARD/FORD

Starting Position:	13
Qualifying Average:	222.867 MPH
Qualifying Speed Rank:	18
Best Practice Speed:	225.242 MPH 5/14
Total Practice Laps:	223
Number Practice Days:	10
Finishing Position:	13
Laps Completed:	193 Accident
Highest Position 1994 Race:	4
Fastest Race Lap:	138 212.455 MPH
1994 Prize Money:	$186,313
INDY 500 Career Earnings:	$993,775
Career INDY 500 Starts:	7
Career Best Finish:	7th 1987

Stan Fox sneaked up on the "500" field, as usual, during the month of May.

He was assigned to a new 1994 Lola with a Ford engine for longtime "500" entrant Ron Hemelgarn. He didn't hit the leader boards during the first week of practice, but when the time came to qualify on Pole Day, he registered a healthy 222.867 mile-an-hour run and made his seventh "500" of the last eight.

"I can be a lot more relaxed when I know the car is fast," Fox said. "It's hard to explain the pressure when the car might be in the last two rows. When you have good equipment, you can worry about the race setup. It makes it that much easier.

"I've been in seven of the last eight (500s). I keep plugging along."

He was the 13th qualifier of the month and started 13th in the lineup. The number 13 would not be that lucky for him, though.

After running as high as fourth on lap #65, he slid and hit the wall in turn #1, bringing out the race's final caution flag. And he finished 13th.

HIRO MATSUSHITA

1994 LOLA/FORD

#22 Panasonic Duskin

Entrant: Simon Racing, Inc.   Crew Chief: Mark Bridges

Starting Position:	18
Qualifying Average:	224.382 MPH
Qualifying Speed Rank:	27
Best Practice Speed:	222.151 5/14
Total Practice Laps:	384
Number Practice Days:	12
Finishing Position:	14
Laps Completed:	193 Running
Highest Position 1994 Race:	14
Fastest Race Lap:	150 205.832 MPH
1994 Prize Money:	$177,013
INDY 500 Career Earnings:	$480,407
Career INDY 500 Starts:	3
Career Best Finish:	14th 1994

Hiro Matsushita returned to the scene as the first Japanese driver ever to qualify for the Indy 500 as a veteran.

Matsushita soldiered through practice uneventfully the first week and recorded his best speed of the month of 222.074 miles an hour in the morning practice session before Pole Day qualifying.

With rain delaying time trials, Matsushita was last away on the first day with just two minutes remaining before the track closed, and recorded a four-lap average of 221.382 to put his machine solidly in the show.

"We went with exactly the same setup as this morning, but the moisture on the track made it a little slow," he said. "The first and last lap, the car had a little push. We have been waiting, waiting, waiting all day. I'm very glad to qualify."

After starting 18th, Matsushita maintained a steady drive and finished 14th, seven laps back.

"The car ran pretty strong most of the day when I was by myself, except in traffic in the corners it would jump and oversteer or understeer, depending on the turbulence of the other cars," he said. "During the race, the air jack didn't work and they had to use the manual jack, so the pit stops were a little slow."

15th PLACE
STEFAN JOHANSSON

#16 Alumax Aluminum

1993 PENSKE/ILMOR

Entrant: Bettenhausen Motorsports   Crew Chief: Steve Ritenour

Starting Position:	27
Qualifying Average:	221.518 MPH
Qualifying Speed Rank:	26
Best Practice Speed:	224.618 MPH 5/14
Total Practice Laps:	391
Number Practice Days:	13
Finishing Position:	15
Laps Completed:	192 Running
Highest Position 1994 Race:	13
Fastest Race Lap:	57 205.479 MPH
1994 Prize Money:	$164,113
INDY 500 Career Earnings:	$350,133
Career INDY 500 Starts:	2
Career Best Finish:	11th 1993

Stefan Johansson returned with the Bettenhausen Associates team, struggled during the first week of practice and got his fastest lap of the month before qualifying on Pole Day morning at 224.618 miles an hour. It was ninth fastest of the morning session and might have predicted a strong qualifying bid.

But the rain delay forced Johansson to the second day, and he waved off his first run after laps at 220.783 and 219.427. Later in the day, with eight minutes remaining in qualifying, he put together a four-lap average of 221.518 to make the field.

"We struggled a little for the first few days," Johansson said. "I think we're up to reasonable speed now. We picked up a huge push in turn #2 that we didn't have in turn #4 during practice right before. We decided before we went out that we'd take 220.5. When you're out there, it doesn't matter if it's 214 or 215, you drive what you can drive."

On Race Day, after starting 27th, Johansson moved up. He was 15th, running at the end, eight laps down.

"This was three hours of torture," he said. "Basically, the car was very loose. It's okay if you're out there by yourself, but as soon as I was in traffic, the car got loose."

1994 LOLA/FORD

#71 PacWest Racing

Entrant: PacWest Racing Group   Crew Chief: Paul Harcus

Starting Position:	17
Qualifying Average:	222.091 MPH
Qualifying Speed Rank:	25
Best Practice Speed:	225.507 MPH 5/14
Total Practice Laps:	619
Number Practice Days:	13
Finishing Position:	16
Laps Completed:	186 Running
Highest Position 1994 Race:	14
Fastest Race Lap:	178 214.572 MPH
1994 Prize Money:	$161,663
INDY 500 Career Earnings:	$161,663
Career INDY 500 Starts:	1
Career Best Finish:	16th 1994

Scott Sharp came to Indianapolis after a distinguished career in the SCCA's Trans Am ranks, with a solid ride with the new PacWest Racing Group team.

By the morning of Pole Day, he was among the 25 drivers who posted their fastest speeds of the month with a lap at 225.507 miles an hour.

At 4:58 p.m. that day, he got his first chance to qualify at the Speedway, and became the 14th to complete a run at an average speed of 222.091 miles an hour.

"I saw my first lap of 222 and, to be honest, I was surprised because the car felt so good," he said. "It just didn't have enough power."

But he felt great. And immediately after his run, he signed a three-year contract with Pacwest.

"It feels fantastic," he said. "Unbelievable...I'm thrilled to be in the field."

On Race Day, he soldiered to a 16th-place finish, battling problems with a gearbox but running at the end.

"That's the longest I've ever gone and my neck is feeling it right now," Sharp said after the race. "We were as fast as anybody after we got back in it. We could have had a top 5, 6, 7, finish. A bit of a shame. The guys worked so hard but what are you going to do?

17th PLACE
EMERSON FITTIPALDI

#2 Marlboro Penske Mercedes
Entrant: Penske Racing, Inc.   **Crew Chief: Rick Rinaman**

1994 PENSKE/MERCEDES BENZ

Starting Position:	3
Qualifying Average:	227.303 MPH
Qualifying Speed Rank:	3
Best Practice Speed:	230.438 MPH 5/12
Total Practice Laps:	893
Number Practice Days:	15
Finishing Position:	17
Laps Completed:	184 Accident
Highest Position 1994 Race:	1
Fastest Race Lap:	121 220.680 MPH
1994 Prize Money:	$298,163
INDY 500 Career Earnings:	$4,042,767
Career INDY 500 Starts:	11
Career Best Finish:	1st 1989, 1993

Emerson Fittipaldi had a picture-perfect month of May...almost.

On his second day of practice, Fittipaldi was second fastest at 226.512 miles an hour. A day later, he was third fastest at 229.264. And on Days #6 and #7, he was at the top of the speed chart at 230.438 and 230.138, respectively.

He seemed an odds-on choice for the pole, but he was also last in the original qualifying line. When rains delayed qualifying, it forced him to make his run on the second day...when it was hotter.

He checked in at 227.303, good for the front row, in third spot, not on the pole.

On Race Day, though, he followed Unser Jr. for 23 laps before taking command in strong fashion. In all, he had 30 of the fastest 50 laps of the race, led for 145 laps and had the fastest race lap of 220.680 on the 121st circuit. As he seemed to be putting the race away, he hit the fourth-turn wall just 16 laps from victory and almost a full lap ahead of Unser Jr., his nearest challenger.

"At that time, I had everything under control and then Al Jr. passed me," Fittipaldi said. "Then, going to turn #4, I just tried to go a little lower than he was. I was two or three cars behind Jr., and I hit the apron, lost the back end and I was about half a foot too low at that time. It was a shame. The car, she was flying. It's a real shame what happened."

1994 LOLA/ILMOR

#28 Indy Regency Racing-Eurosport
Entrant: Indy Regency Racing   Crew Chief: John Jackson

Starting Position:	8
Qualifying Average:	223.673 MPH
Qualifying Speed Rank:	10
Best Practice Speed:	225.983 MPH 5/12
Total Practice Laps:	198
Number Practice Days:	12
Finishing Position:	18
Laps Completed:	179 Engine
Highest Position 1994 Race:	4
Fastest Race Lap:	5 211.060 MPH
1994 Prize Money:	$161,412
INDY 500 Career Earnings:	$2,933,249
Career INDY 500 Starts:	10
Career Best Finish:	1st 1990

Arie Luyendyk came to Indy with a new team, Indy Regency Racing, and a new hope to repeat his 1990 "500" victory.

It took awhile to work out the bugs, but Luyendyk was ninth fastest in practice two days before Pole Day at 225.983 miles an hour.

"I'm not trying to get crazy and mix it up with the Penskes and the other teams that are on top," he said. "We just have to do the best job we can and I know the team is doing the best job it can do."

When qualifying came, Luyendyk became the 11th qualifier of Pole Day, checking in at 223.673 miles an hour after starting off with a 225-plus lap.

"The run started out great," he said. "I ran a 225 but then the car got loose and the speed dropped to 224. I just tried to maintain my run. I had problems with my valve. It didn't want to close so I was running with only 43 inches of boost on the last lap."

The run was good for eighth starting position.

He started fast, moving to fourth spot at lap #17 and hovered in the top 10 through the 125-mile mark before falling back. Engine failure ended his day in 18th place after 179 laps.

Luyendyk was brief. "After it went yellow, the engine blew up," he said.

19th PLACE
LYN ST. JAMES

1994 LOLA/FORD

#90 Spirit Of The American Woman-JCPenney/Reebok/Lee
Entrant: Dick Simon Racing, Inc.   Crew Chief: Emory Donaldson

Starting Position:	6
Qualifying Average:	224.154 MPH
Qualifying Speed Rank:	6
Best Practice Speed:	225.745 MPH 5/13
Total Practice Laps:	353
Number Practice Days:	12
Finishing Position:	19
Laps Completed:	170 Running
Highest Position 1994 Race:	10
Fastest Race Lap:	77 211.655 MPH
1994 Prize Money:	$161,212
INDY 500 Career Earnings:	$495,568
Career INDY 500 Starts:	3
Career Best Finish:	11th 1992

Lyn St. James came to Indy as a veteran looking to improve her past performances.

She built up speed quietly the first the week, and when her turn came on Pole Day, when others' speeds were off, she chalked up a four-lap average at 224.154 miles an hour. It was good for sixth starting spot, the highest ever for a woman driver at Indy, and outqualified both Nigel Mansell and Mario Andretti.

"It feels really good," St. James said. "I parked my emotions when I crawled into the race car and just felt what the car was doing. I'm dying to see a tape of the run. I know I came closer to the wall than I have all week. The emotions came back when I drove into the pits after qualifying and saw my crew members and even some competitors congratulating me."

On Race Day, she had problems and got caught up in an accident, but was still running at the finish and wound up 19th.

"I'm not sure who hit me but it damaged my left front suspension," St. James said. "I locked the brakes but couldn't get by. But I can't complain too much. I finished the race. You have no idea how the car is going to feel once it's repaired, so it was an awkward race for me. I just tried to hang in there."

SCOTT BRAYTON

1993 LOLA/MENARD

#59 Glidden Paint Special
Entrant: Team Menard, Inc.   Crew Chief: Terry Day

Starting Position:	23
Qualifying Average:	223.652 MPH
Qualifying Speed Rank:	11
Best Practice Speed:	227.658 MPH 5/8
Total Practice Laps:	411
Number Practice Days:	11
Finishing Position:	20
Laps Completed:	116 Engine
Highest Position 1994 Race:	5
Fastest Race Lap:	53 212.696 MPH
1994 Prize Money:	$177,112
INDY 500 Career Earnings:	$1,681,514
Career INDY 500 Starts:	13
Career Best Finish:	6th 1989, 1993

Scott Brayton, in his first ride with Team Menard, hoped to make his 13th straight Indy 500 field — which is the longest consecutive streak among active drivers except for Mario Andretti.

He went to the top of the speed charts on the first day at 227.658 miles an hour and stayed in the top 10 much of the first week.

On Pole Day he waved off after three laps in the 221-mile-an-hour bracket. Later, he waved off after a 220-plus and 221-plus in a backup machine. On the second day, he waved off after a 223-plus lap in a third car. With 15 minutes to go, he qualified the backup machine to teammate Eddie Cheever at a four-lap average of 223.652.

"I'm happy to be in the field after four times," Brayton said. "I'm relieved. My first lap was the quickest and I cooked the tires on that lap. Then my times dropped. The team did a fantastic job. They pulled the car apart and set it up for me. They had to change seating because I'm real short and Eddie's so tall. It was a great effort."

On Race Day, after starting 23rd, Brayton reached as high as fifth on the 116th lap after moving up through the field. His day ended when the engine failed.

"The motor broke...just one of those things," Brayton said. "We were where we needed to be."

21st PLACE
RAUL BOESEL

#5 Duracell Charger

1994 LOLA/FORD

Entrant: Dick Simon Racing, Inc.   Crew Chief: Brad McCanless

Starting Position:	2
Qualifying Average:	227.618 MPH
Qualifying Speed Rank:	2
Best Practice Speed:	230.403 MPH 5/10
Total Practice Laps:	495
Number Practice Days:	12
Finishing Position:	21
Laps Completed:	100 Water Pump
Highest Position 1994 Race:	2
Fastest Race Lap:	12 210.261 MPH
1994 Prize Money:	$173,112
INDY 500 Career Earnings:	$1,421,680
Career INDY 500 Starts:	8
Career Best Finish:	3rd 1989

Raul Boesel experienced one of his most impressive months of May from the start.

On day #4, he became the first to reach 230 miles an hour with a lap at 230.403 and seemed to be a contender to challenge the Penskes for the pole.

He was sixth to take the track for a qualifying run on Pole Day and put together a four-lap average of 227.618, the fastest run at the time. He was on the pole for 28 minutes before Al Unser Jr., pushed him back to second.

"I enjoy this place very well," Boesel said. "This morning, I thought I had a shot at the pole. I was

relaxed and the car was very good. I was pretty confident this morning. The car was perfect."

On Race Day, he dropped to seventh on the first lap and hovered in the bottom half of the top 10 before making his move. He was second on lap #66 to Emerson Fittipaldi. Although he was a lap down at the time, he was still in the top 10 when a water pump failure ended his day and he finished 21st.

"The car was losing water from the engine," Boesel said. "From the start, the car wasn't producing the normal amount of power. I was hoping to hang in there and finish the race, but I guess that didn't happen."

22nd PLACE
NIGEL MANSELL

#1 Kmart Texaco Havoline Newman/Haas Racing
Entrant: Newman/Haas Racing   Crew Chief: Tom Wurtz

Starting Position:	7
Qualifying Average:	224.041 MPH
Qualifying Speed Rank:	8
Best Practice Speed:	228.137 MPH
Total Practice Laps:	514
Number Practice Days:	9
Finishing Position:	22
Laps Completed:	92 Accident
Highest Position 1994 Race:	3
Fastest Race Lap:	91 216.549 MPH
1994 Prize Money:	$153,312
INDY 500 Career Earnings:	$544,615
Career INDY 500 Starts:	2
Career Best Finish:	3rd 1993

Nigel Mansell had a different month of May from his outstanding first-year performance of 1993 when he overcame a back injury and nearly won.

He jumped into the top 10 on the third day of practice and was second to Al Unser Jr. on the fourth day with a lap at 225.807. When Pole Day came, he was fastest of the morning practice at 228.137, his best lap of the month.

But he was the 17th to attempt qualification at 1:45 p.m. and his four-lap average was 224.041.

"I am as happy as anything," Mansell said. "We qualified, we beat the weather and we're in. I'm delighted. I'm sitting here, I'm comfortable, I'm not in pain and I'm in the race."

The run left him starting seventh in the lineup for Race Day. He moved to third on lap #92 and had three of the day's fastest race laps before a peculiar accident left him with a 22nd-place finish.

Mansell and Dennis Vitolo tangled in the aftermath of the day's fourth caution flag, Vitolo's car coming to rest atop Mansell's, and a fire started.

"The car just ran over the top of him," said Tom Wurtz, Mansell's chief mechanic. "He got out on his own, so we hope he's okay."

"I feel great," Mansell said. "I have a concussion. I'm very upset. I've never seen anything like that before."

23rd PLACE
PAUL TRACY

#3 Marlboro Penske Mercedes
Entrant: Penske Racing, Inc.   Crew Chief: Jon Bouslog

1994 PENSKE/MERCEDES BENZ

Starting Position:	25
Qualifying Average:	222.710 MPH
Qualifying Speed Rank:	19
Best Practice Speed:	229.961 MPH 5/10
Total Practice Laps:	553
Number Practice Days:	11
Finishing Position:	23
Laps Completed:	92 Turbocharger
Highest Position 1994 Race:	12
Fastest Race Lap:	13 213.680 MPH
1994 Prize Money:	$151,612
INDY 500 Career Earnings:	$447,668
Career INDY 500 Starts:	3
Career Best Finish:	20th 1992

Paul Tracy came to Indy as a member of the Penske team with the Mercedes engines that caused much speculation on pit road.

He fueled the speculation by being second fastest on three different days of practice. On the last day before qualifying, Tracy got loose in turn #3 nd slammed the outside wall in turn #4, getting him a trip to Methodist Hospital for an overnight stay and out of competition for the pole position.

He was released from Methodist on Pole Day morning. When teammate Fittipaldi was last to qualify from the original line on Sunday, Al Unser Jr.'s backup car was in line for Tracy. But he waved off after two laps at 222-plus and a third at 220-plus. Two hours later, he qualified at 222.710, good for 25th starting spot.

"I felt I could have been able to run yesterday but the doctors didn't want me to," Tracy said. "I just got to keep on truckin'. I just have to concentrate on the race and not look behind me. I feel fine. I've raced in worse condition than this. I probably race my best when I'm a little bit hurt."

On Race Day, his problems started early and a blown turbocharger ended his day after 92 laps for a 23rd-place finish.

"It was still running when I came in," Tracy said. "I was trying to work my way up slowly, no risky moves. I was disappointed."

1993 LOLA/FORD

#99 Beck Motorsports /Simon Racing

Entrant: Beck Motorsports/Simon Racing   Crew Chief: Greg Beck

Starting Position:	14
Qualifying Average:	222.545 MPH
Qualifying Speed Rank:	21
Best Practice Speed:	222.646 MPH 5/14
Total Practice Laps:	254
Number Practice Days:	8
Finishing Position:	24
Laps Completed:	90 Accident
Highest Position 1994 Race:	7
Fastest Race Lap:	12 211.173 MPH
1994 Prize Money:	$150,362
INDY 500 Career Earnings:	$150,362
Career INDY 500 Starts:	1
Career Best Finish:	24th 1994

Hideshi Matsuda was making the effort to go from television commentator to race driver at the "500."

Matsuda had a Dick Simon-prepared car fielded by Beck Motorsports, and his first duty was to participate in Simon's annual "first on the track" show. Sitting on the pit wall behind his cars on opening day, the Simon "production" was explained to him.

He was asked if he was ready. "yes, of course," he said with a smile, not needing his interpreter.

He drew the No. 1 qualifying spot to be first up when the first day of time trials arrived.

He recorded an average of 222.545 miles an hour, with a fastest lap of 222.646. Both one-lap and four-lap marks were the fastest ever turned in by a rookie at Indy...at the time.

"Surprised," he said when asked his reaction. "Very happy, but a little disappointed since I ran faster in practice. It's just like a dream. Two years ago, I came as a reporter. Then I decided to race here. It's the happiest moment of my life."

On Race Day, his dream ended after his 90th lap, when he spun and banged the wall in turn #2 to bring out the fourth cautio flag.

He had a bruised left leg and finished 24th, but he had made a big transition and a spot in Speedway history.

25th PLACE
JOHN PAUL, JR.

#45 CYBERGENICS/Team Losi/Pro Formance
Entrant: Pro Formance Motorsports   Crew Chief: Randy Bain

1993 LOLA/ILMOR

Starting Position:	30
Qualifying Average:	222.500 MPH
Qualifying Speed Rank:	22
Best Practice Speed:	223.109 MPH 5/14
Total Practice Laps:	659
Number Practice Days:	12
Finishing Position:	25
Laps Completed:	90 Accident
Highest Position 1994 Race:	16
Fastest Race Lap:	56 208.754 MPH
1994 Prize Money:	$150,362
INDY 500 Career Earnings:	$671,293
Career INDY 500 Starts:	5
Career Best Finish:	10th 1992

John Paul Jr. started the month with the Pro Formance team and followed his traditional path of being a strong second weekend qualifier.

He turned his fastest practice lap of the month at 223.109 the morning of Pole Day, but when his turn came, he could muster only a first lap at 218-plus and two more at 220-plus and the team waved off the run. On the second day, the team waved off again after three laps at 219-plus.

On Day #13, two days before the final weekend of qualifications was to begin, Paul Jr. turned a lap at 222.058, tops among drivers yet to qualify. He was fastest again on Day #14 and was the first qualifier out on the third qualifying day. He registered a four-lap run of 222.500 to go solidly into the show.

"We've had the speed," he said. "It's never easy here. We're just thankful to be here. I really love this place. I was really happy. I stood on it and it got better and better."

In the race, Paul Jr. was the victim of an unfortunate circumstance and finished 25th after completing 89 laps.

"(Hideshi) Matsuda crashed first," he said. "I ran over something of his and I spun. Me and Michael Andretti were trying to catch up to the pace car."

26th PLACE
DENNIS VITOLO

1993 LOLA/FORD

#79 Hooligan's/Carlo/Charter America/Dick Simon Racing
Entrant: Dick Simon Racing, Inc.   Crew Chief: Peter Jacobs

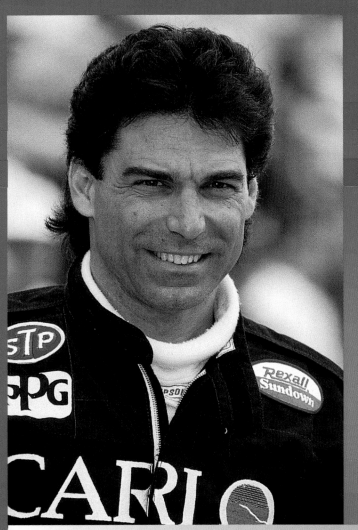

Starting Position:	15
Qualifying Average:	222.439 MPH
Qualifying Speed Rank:	23
Best Practice Speed:	222.954 MPH 5/14
Total Practice Laps:	420
Number Practice Days:	7
Finishing Position:	26
Laps Completed:	89 Accident
Highest Position 1994 Race:	16
Fastest Race Lap:	68 204.592 MPH
1994 Prize Money:	$143,862
INDY 500 Career Earnings:	$143,862
Career INDY 500 Starts:	1
Career Best Finish:	26th 1994

Dennis Vitolo started his month of May as part of the Dick Simon stable and was second to Raul Boesel coming off pit road in Simon's annual "first-on-the-track" derby.

Later on that first day, he completed the observation phase of his driver's test and was ready to go.

He posted his fastest lap of practice on Pole Day morning at 221.261 and made the eighth qualification attempt of the month as time trials started.

He recorded a four-lap average of 222.439 with a top lap of 222.954 to set a new one-lap record for rookie drivers.

"By far, my best run so far," Vitolo said. "I had a little push but I was thrilled with my run."

He gave Simon credit for bringing him along as a driver.

"From Day #1, Dick has been there," he said. "As a rookie, I wanted to come and run for Simon. From ROP on, he coached me as a driver. It's because of him I'm here today."

In the race, after starting 15th, he wound up 26th, the victim of a strange turn #3 accident in which he wound up on top of Nigel Mansell's car.

"The car was good at the beginning but it kept getting looser and looser," Vitolo said. "This is racing. I can't blame anybody but myself."

27th PLACE
MARCO GRECO

#25 Int Sports LTD
Entrant: Arciero Project Indy/Simon   **Crew Chief: Barry Brooke**

1994 LOLA/FORD

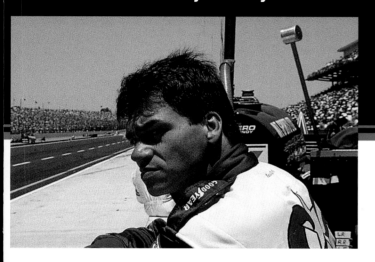

Starting Position:	32
Qualifying Average:	221.216 MPH
Qualifying Speed Rank:	31
Best Practice Speed:	221.751 MPH 5/22
Total Practice Laps:	534
Number Practice Days:	9
Finishing Position:	27
Laps Completed:	53 Electrical
Highest Position 1994 Race:	21
Fastest Race Lap:	18 202.070 MPH
1994 Prize Money:	$171,762
INDY 500 Career Earnings:	$171,762
Career INDY 500 Starts:	1
Career Best Finish:	27th 1994

Marco Greco joined the Brazilian contingent at Indy, campaigning an Arciero Project Indy entry prepared by Dick Simon Racing.

On his first qualifying attempt on Pole Day, he waved off after laps at 214 and 215. He reached 220 mph to become fourth fastest of non-qualified drivers on Day #13, two days before the final qualifying weekend, but few thought it would be enough.

Although he had his fastest speed in practice on the morning of the third qualifying day, he mustered only a top lap of 218.616 on his second qualifying run and waved off. But, with two strikes, Greco rolled away at 5:35 p.m., only 25 minutes before the close of qualifying on the final day, and pushed the car to a four-lap average of 221.216 to bump Scott Goodyear from the field.

"We saved the tires that I ran 219 on this morning and the car was perfect," Greco said. "I had to slack off a little bit. I was worried about the popoff valve going off in turn #4. It was really tough to just watch all day. That was the toughest part, but I was so happy to be here."

On Race Day, electrical failure ended his race after 53 laps and he finished 27th.

"It was a bent valve that stopped us from running and we also had an electrical problem," he said. "I felt the bent valve from the start. The whole crew worked very hard to put me in the show. I'll be back next year."

77

1994 REYNARD/ILMOR

#7 Tecate/Quaker State/Reynard/Ilmor

Entrant: Galles Racing International   Crew Chief: Mitch Davis

Starting Position:	26
Qualifying Average:	222.657 MPH
Qualifying Speed Rank:	20
Best Practice Speed:	224.629 MPH 5/13
Total Practice Laps:	691
Number Practice Days:	12
Finishing Position:	28
Laps Completed:	30 Suspension
Highest Position 1994 Race:	15
Fastest Race Lap:	19 211.745 MPH
1994 Prize Money:	$146,612
INDY 500 Career Earnings:	$146,612
Career INDY 500 Starts:	1
Career Best Finish:	28th 1994

Adrian Fernandez came to Indy as the rookie solo driver for the Galles team, which had a history at Indy.

He passed the final observation phase of the required driver's test on the first day of practice and went about preparing to qualify.

He didn't crack the top 10 in practice during the first week and as the seventh to make a qualifying attempt, waved off after a lap at 218-plus. On the second day, he put together a smooth run — the laps ranged between 222.217 and 222.949 — for a four-lap average of 222.657, strongly in the show.

"It's a relief to qualify," Fernandez said. "Yesterday, I was completely frustrated. I was very nervous but once I did the first lap, I felt good. Today, there was a little more pressure. Everyone was slowing down dramatically. We did some changes today that helped us. I knew I had to do a consistent run of 222 to be safe for the race."

Fernandez started 26th, but suspension failure ended his day after just 30 laps and he finished 28th.

But in his brief run, he had reached as high as 15th.

29th PLACE
DOMINIC DOBSON

#17 PacWest Racing
Entrant: PacWest Racing Group   Crew Chief: David Luckett

1994 LOLA/FORD

Starting Position:	12
Qualifying Average:	222.970 MPH
Qualifying Speed Rank:	17
Best Practice Speed:	225.598 MPH 5/14
Total Practice Laps:	588
Number Practice Days:	12
Finishing Position:	29
Laps Completed:	29 Accident
Highest Position 1994 Race:	11
Fastest Race Lap:	20 211.436 MPH
1994 Prize Money:	$139,912
INDY 500 Career Earnings:	$962,867
Career INDY 500 Starts:	7
Career Best Finish:	12th 1992

Dominic Dobson came to Indianapolis with the new PacWest Racing Group team, a welcome change from past years' tradition of jumping in a car the second week of practice.

Although he didn't crack the top 10 during the week, the PacWest group worked to sort out the machines of Dobson and teammate Scott Sharp. In the morning practice session on Pole Day, Dobson reached 225.598, 10th fastest of the session.

In qualifying, he was fourth out and became the third qualifier of the first day at 222.970.

"The speed in the first lap felt really good," Dobson said. "It feels much better than last year.

The track does change with the rain, but I'm safely in now. This morning, conditions were ideal. I had my foot down as much as I could. I was starting to pick up understeering on the second lap. We have a good mechanical setup, even with the turbulent air."

He started 12th on Race Day, but his run ended early when he and Mike Groff tangled in turn #1. He finished 29th after completing 29 laps and the accident left him with bruised legs.

"I couldn't tell exactly what happened," Dobson said. "I passed Hideshi (Matsuda) and came inside Groff in turn #1 and there wasn't enough room. I'm not sure if Hideshi was involved."

1994 LOLA/FORD

#40 Budweiser King Racing

Entrant: Kenny Bernstein's Budweiser King   Crew Chief: Chris Griffis

Starting Position:	33
Qualifying Average:	223.817 MPH
Qualifying Speed Rank:	9
Best Practice Speed:	225.762 MPH 5/14
Total Practice Laps:	824
Number Practice Days:	14
Finishing Position:	30
Laps Completed:	29 Mechanical
Highest Position 1994 Race:	22
Fastest Race Lap:	18 201.414 MPH
1994 Prize Money:	$159,312
INDY 500 Career Earnings:	$1,253,359
Career INDY 500 Starts:	5
Career Best Finish:	2nd 1992

Scott Goodyear came to Indy for the first time with Kenny Bernstein's King Motorsports team.

He was the fifth driver out when qualifications opened, but waved off after three laps in the 221-222 bracket. He was second out on the second day of time trials in his backup machine, still with a shot at a good starting spot, but waved off after laps of 216-plus and 218-plus.

The team threw a full-fledged assault on the problems during the second week of practice and Davy Jones practiced Goodyear's backup car as a protective "cushion" to get the team in the field.

Goodyear was second to qualify on the third day with a four-lap average of 220.737. Jones found speed and qualified later in the day at 223.817.

With 25 minutes left in qualifying on the final day, Marco Greco bumped Goodyear from the field. After a week of procedural moves, the team put Goodyear in Jones' qualified machine for Race Day.

But luck eluded Goodyear, as mechanical problems sidelined him in 30th position after just 29 laps.

"I got caught up in the (Groff-Dobson) accident and then had motor problems," Goodyear said. "We didn't expect it because it was a fresh motor. The team has been to hell and back this month. We've been very competitive the last few years and it's just hard to take."

31st PLACE
MIKE GROFF

#10 Motorola
Entrant: Rahal/Hogan Racing   Crew Chief: Larry Ellert

1993 PENSKE/ILMOR C+

Starting Position:	31
Qualifying Average:	221.355 MPH
Qualifying Speed Rank:	28
Best Practice Speed:	224.143 MPH 5/21
Total Practice Laps:	581
Number Practice Days:	13
Finishing Position:	31
Laps Completed:	28 Accident
Highest Position 1994 Race:	21
Fastest Race Lap:	18 200.790 MPH
1994 Prize Money:	$138,812
INDY 500 Career Earnings:	$297,102
Career INDY 500 Starts:	2
Career Best Finish:	24th 1991

Mike Groff came to the Speedway after being the "test pilot" for the new Honda engine for the Rahal-Hogan team.

His month started ominously with an apparent engine failure and a trip into the first-turn wall on Day #3 of the month. Groff was uninjured and on Pole Day he qualified ninth at an average speed of 218.808. It was the slowest qualification attempt of the weekend and the Rahal-Hogan team announced the following Tuesday that it had acquired a pair of 1993 Penskes with Ilmor engines in case its qualified entries were too slow.

"I'm not super comfortable in it, but we'll work on it tonight," Groff said. "It's a great car. Roger (Penske) gave us a great opportunity and this car'll get it done."

When Davy Jones bumped Groff from the field on the third qualifying day, the Rahal-Hogan team withdrew the qualified car and had the Penske next in line. Groff turned four comfortable laps at an average of 221.355 and joined the field.

"Getting in the Penske car was a nice surprise," Groff said. "I think we're safe."

On Race Day, Groff started and finished 31st, victim of an accident when he and Dominic Dobson tangled in turn #1.

"We were feeling not too bad," Groff said. "In turn #1, a couple of cars came up behind me. Someone popped me from behind, which was not too good."

32nd PLACE
MARIO ANDRETTI

#6 Kmart Texaco Havoline Newman/Haas Racing
Entrant: Newman/Haas Racing   Crew Chief: John Simmons

Starting Position:	9
Qualifying Average:	223.503 MPH
Qualifying Speed Rank:	12
Best Practice Speed:	228.606 MPH 5/14
Total Practice Laps:	587
Number Practice Days:	13
Finishing Position:	32
Laps Completed:	23 Fuel System
Highest Position 1994 Race:	4
Fastest Race Lap:	14 210.684 MPH
1994 Prize Money:	$138,512
INDY 500 Career Earnings:	$2,766,931
Career INDY 500 Starts:	29
Career Best Finish:	1st 1969

Mario Andretti came to Indy as a driver for the last time, having announced his retirement effective at the end of the 1994 season. In his long and storied career, he wanted one more victory here to match his 1969 triumph.

He was sixth fastest on Day #1 at 223.753 and stayed in the top 10 every day of the first week. He ran his fastest lap of the month at 228.606 in the morning practice before Pole Day qualifying.

He drew a late number in line, and when rain delayed qualifying, he was forced to qualify on Sunday. He was first out and registered an average of 223.503, good for ninth starting spot for his final "500."

"We were set up for these conditions but we knew we'd struggle," Andretti said. "Yesterday, with those conditions, my car was super. You can put the order in, but no one listens. The conditions are such that we can't control it. I knew I had a real shot at the front row. The car was good in the morning, when I did 228."

On Race Day, he got a big drop on his competition, gaining four spots to fifth on the first lap. He stayed there and eventually moved to fourth at 50 miles. But the fuel system failed on his machine and he was the second driver to go to the sidelines.

"Disappointed," he said. "We have a long way to go. The support of the team is phenomenal. When I win, they win. When I lose, they lose."

33rd PLACE
ROBERTO GUERRERO

#21 Interstate Batteries/Pagan Racing

1992 LOLA/BUICK

Entrant: Pagan Racing, Inc.   Crew Chief: John Barnes

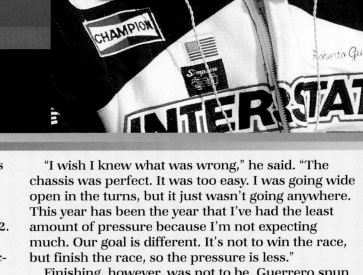

Starting Position:	20
Qualifying Average:	221.278 MPH
Qualifying Speed Rank:	30
Best Practice Speed:	226.637 MPH 5/14
Total Practice Laps:	428
Number Practice Days:	13
Finishing Position:	33
Laps Completed:	20 Accident
Highest Position 1994 Race:	19
Fastest Race Lap:	12 211.506 MPH
1994 Prize Money:	$143,912
INDY 500 Career Earnings:	$1,680,057
Career INDY 500 Starts:	10
Career Best Finish:	2nd 1984, 1987

Roberto Guerrero found reason for nostalgia as the month of May opened.

He was driving the Interstate Batteries/Pagan Racing entries, and his primary car was the 1992 model Lola in which he set the track record in 1992.

Guerrero was second fastest on Day #2 of the month, which turned out to be the first day of practice, with a lap at 225.558 miles an hour. He was fifth fastest on the second day at 225.739.

When Pole Day arrived, Guerrero went out 10 minutes from the close of the day and registered a solid four-lap average of 221.278. It turned out to be the only 1992 model car to make the "500" field.

"I wish I knew what was wrong," he said. "The chassis was perfect. It was too easy. I was going wide open in the turns, but it just wasn't going anywhere. This year has been the year that I've had the least amount of pressure because I'm not expecting much. Our goal is different. It's not to win the race, but finish the race, so the pressure is less."

Finishing, however, was not to be. Guerrero spun in the south short chute and hit the wall in turn #2 to bring out the race's second caution flag.

"It caught me totally by surprise," he said. "Everything was running smoothly. For no reason, the back end came around. I just don't know."

FOR THOSE WHO TRIED

There is a great deal more to the Indianapolis 500 than merely the race itself. Many feel that the qualification procedure alone constitutes a separate event unto itself. Forty-one drivers attempted to earn one of 33 starting positions, eight came up short and eight more were forced to the sidelines by having practiced without making any qualifying attempt at all. This is a salute to their valiant efforts.

Davy Jones qualified at 223.817 mph for the Budweiser King team but ended up as a spectator on Race Day. When teammate Scott Goodyear's speed did not hold up as one of the 33 fastest, Jones was obliged to turn his car over to Goodyear.

In 78 runnings of the Indianapolis 500, there has never been a Smith in the lineup. Mark Smith, 34th fastest in time trials one year ago was 35th in 1994. He hit the wall in trying to qualify a backup car in the closing minutes of time trials.

The qualifying speeds of Mike Groff and Bobby Rahal in Honda-powered cars were not quite fast enough to make the field, forcing Rahal to lease two Ilmor-powered machines from Roger Penske in order to get his team in the show.

Willy T. Ribbs was not quite able to crack the toughest Indy 500 starting field in years. It wasn't for lack of trying.

Everybody was disappointed when fan favorite Gary Bettenhausen failed to make the field, driving for younger brother Tony.

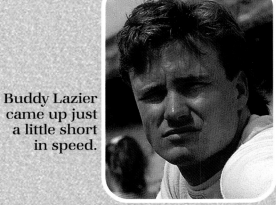

Buddy Lazier came up just a little short in speed.

Geoff Brabham's assignment to the third Menard entry came late in the month but stamped him a certain qualifier. He didn't miss by much.

For Those Who Tried

Didier Theys tried to get a full month's work done in a day and a half but ran out of time.

Jeff Andretti did not go to the qualifying line with the second Hemelgarn entry.

Pancho Carter decided not to make a qualifying attempt on the final weekend.

The Greenfield family's experimental engine had very little track time with Johnny Parsons at the wheel.

When the French-backed team of Stephan Gregoire was withdrawn, he practiced briefly with the Simon and McCormack teams.

Tero Palmroth tried unsuccessfully to qualify the car vacated by retiree Al Unser. Roberto Moreno, who hadn't been to the Speedway since 1986, also spent some practice time in Unser's car.

Al Unser surprised just about everybody by announcing his retirement after the first weekend of qualifications.

The Riley & Scott team arrived with a three-year-old car piloted by Jim Crawford, but didn't achieve qualifying speed.

Before The Roar

Undoubtedly goosebumps arise when Mrs. Hulman utters those famous words and the roar of 33 engines fills the air on Race morning. "Before The Roar" chronicles the events leading up to that magic moment at the World's Most Famous Race Course.

THE

by Gordon Kirby

All month everyone asked if it was possible to beat the Mercedes-Benz-powered Penskes driven by Al Unser Jr., Emerson Fittipaldi and Paul Tracy. The Penskes were quickest on most days of practice and all three drivers ran relentlessly, day after day, putting more than 4,000 miles on their new Mercedes 500I engines. Fittipaldi turned the fastest practice lap of the month and Unser qualified on the pole with Fittipaldi on the outside of the front row. Come race day, the answer to the big question of 1994 turned out to be a resounding no as Fittipaldi and Unser dominated the 78th running of the 500.

1994 RACE

Unser led the opening laps before Fittipaldi took control. The two-time winner edged steadily, inexorably away from Unser and looked like he might win handily until he crashed, almost inexplicably, while trying to lap Unser with just fifteen laps to go. Fittipaldi's misfortune handed the 78th Indianapolis 500 to teammate Unser who took the checkered flag under the yellow after Stan Fox crashed with just four laps to go. It was Unser's second win at Indianapolis - the ninth for his family - and Penske's tenth, a record for any team.

93

The weather for this year's 500 was darn near perfect - sunny and warm with a light breeze from the south. All month the weather cooperated in uncommonly delightful style with precious little rain and a refreshing lack of humidity. For race day to be equally pleasant seemed a blessing from heaven, a prelude to a 500 which would unfold with few incidents and only one minor foot injury.

The start was surprisingly ragged with Unser and Fittipaldi leaping ahead as fellow front row starter Raul Boesel fell to seventh and Michael Andretti surged into third place. "I think it was a bad start," commented Boesel. "The cars were not lined up properly and it took a long time to wave the green flag. The Penskes just accelerated so much faster out of turn four, I thought they wouldn't give us the green."

Second row starter Andretti found Boesel in his way and had to get out of the throttle to avoid passing him before the green flag waved. "I was backing off the throttle because I didn't want to pass Raul before the

THE 1994 RACE

starter waved the flag," said Michael. "The Penskes criss-crossed and went both ways around Raul so he had to get out of the throttle. Then I just got on it and went."

Through the opening laps Michael was the only driver to keep Unser and Fittipaldi in sight chased by 1990 winner Arie Luyendyk, Mario Andretti, Cheever, impressive rookie Villeneuve, Mansell and Boesel. Luyendyk made a great start from the third row but was soon in trouble as his car started to get increasingly tail-happy. As Arie began to lose ground the first yellow of the race came out when Roberto Guerrero spun and clouted the wall. Guerrero was uninjured but the yellow brought everyone in for the first round of pit stops for fuel and tires.

Just after the restart there was a two-car accident in turn one when Dominic Dobson and Mike Groff got together as they jockeyed for position. Both cars clouted the wall and Groff was lucky to escape with nothing worse than a cracked bone in his left foot. In the immediate aftermath of the accident Lyn St. James ran into the back of Scott Goodyear's car, ending Goodyear's race and bringing St. James into the pits for lengthy repairs.

Also in trouble during this yellow was Mario Andretti who pulled into the pits with a fuel system problem. An attempt was made to effect repairs but the problem was deep inside Mario's engine and his 29th and final start at Indianapolis came to an ignominious end. Andretti made a great start and was a very strong fifth through the opening laps. You had to feel deep misery for his and his family's unending poor luck at the Speedway.

"We were competitive," said a deeply disappointed Andretti. "We were pretty much where I was hoping I would be at this point. Just a couple of little adjustments in the car and we would have been right there. We were definitely in the ball park. All the possibilities were still with us, very loud and clear, but it just wasn't meant to be I guess."

100 MILES

Pos.	Car No.	Driver
1	2	Emerson Fittipaldi
2	31	Al Unser, Jr.
3	27	Eddie Cheever
4	8	Michael Andretti
5	33	John Andretti
6	1	Nigel Mansell
7	5	Raul Boesel
8	18	Jimmy Vasser
9	9	Robby Gordon
10	28	Arie Luyendyk

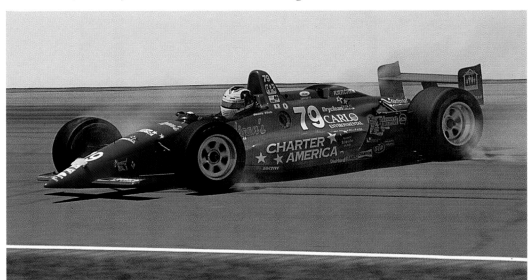

Rookie Dennis Vitolo miraculously misses the wall doing a 360 degree spin on lap #6.

An ignition problem ends Mario Andretti's Indy 500 career in frustration.

There was a long delay to remove the wreckage from the multi-car incident which caused the yellow and on the restart Michael Andretti hit trouble. He had cut a tire on debris from the accident and had to come into the pits under the green, losing a lap. Then there were a couple of stop and go penalties handed out to Cheever and Mansell respectively for passing Boesel under the yellow in the pits.

So it was that Fittipaldi and Unser began to take complete control of the race with only John Andretti hounding them. Andretti moved up steadily from the fourth row and ran a strong third for some time before he too found his car getting ever more tail-happy. After seventy of the 200 laps therefore, the only car to remain unlapped by Fittipaldi and Unser was rookie Villeneuve.

THE 1994 RACE

200 MILES

Pos.	Car No.	Driver
1	2	Emerson Fittipaldi
2	31	Al Unser, Jr.
3	12	Jacques Villeneuve
4	4	Bobby Rahal
5	18	Jimmy Vasser
6	59	Scott Brayton
7	1	Nigel Mansell
8	9	Robby Gordon
9	5	Raul Boesel
10	33	John Andretti

Through the middle stages of the race the day belonged entirely to Fittipaldi who led his teammate by half a lap and more for much of the distance. In fact, Fittipaldi led 145 of the 200 laps and appeared to have the race in the bag when he crashed with fifteen laps to go. Fittipaldi was directly behind Unser at the time. A few laps earlier he had lapped Unser but then Al Jr. unlapped himself and after two more laps, Fittipaldi crashed hard in the fourth turn.

"I'm very disappointed," commented Fittipaldi. "At that time I had everything under control. The car was flying. I nearly corrected it but it was too late. Going into turn four I tried to go a little lower than Jr. and hit the apron. I hit the corrugation (rumble strips). I was about half a foot too low. It's really a shame that happened. We should have been one-two."

Top; Rookie star Jacques Villeneuve impresses everyone with his ability to run up front. Below; Emerson Fittipaldi took charge in the pits and on the track.

Dominic Dobson
and Mike Groff
tangle in turn #1
as the rest of the
field scramble to
avoid the debris.

Winner Unser said he thought Fittipaldi lost control in the turbulence behind his car. "He got caught up in my turbulence," explained Unser. "He was trying hard to lap me and I was trying extremely hard to keep from being passed. The lap before the same thing happened to me. I had to get him on the brakes and almost caught the wall. He took a run on me and I saw him hit the fence. I felt bad for a second!"

Unser noted that the track was extremely slippery outside the groove. "I got a little bit into the gray about half-distance," commented Unser. "And it's like a vacuum out there. It'll suck you right into the wall."

Team owner Roger Penske said that Fittipaldi was trying to lap Unser because he thought he might have to stop for a final splash of fuel with a

handful of laps to go while Unser might have been able to run to the finish without stopping. The yellow for Fittipaldi's accident made this a moot point, enabling Unser to run easily to the checkered flag without any thoughts of stopping for a splash of fuel.

Unser's victory was his second in the last three years at Indianapolis and the ninth for the Unser family. It also was the third time in the last three years and tenth time overall that one of Roger Penske's cars has won the Indianapolis 500 as well as being a remarkable debut win for Mercedes-Benz's 500I push-rod V8.

"It was really a great run all day," said Unser. "We had been working on the car to make it better. I think Emerson was the strongest player out there. His car was working really well but mine was understeering, particularly when I was running in traffic. We kept giving it more front wing but we never really got the front to stick.

"Then on my last set of tires the stagger went away and my car was as bad as it had been all day. I got stuck behind a purple car and couldn't make any ground. Emerson just closed it right down and came back and lapped me. I was trying extremely hard when I passed him back and unlapped myself and I know he was trying hard to keep me behind him."

Unser said Fittipaldi was doing the right thing by trying to maintain a lap's lead on him. "If you've got a heavy hitter in front of you, you do everything you can to lap him. It would have put the final nail in my coffin if he could have done that."

As well as fighting a push or understeer all day, Unser also had trouble with his radio. For most of the race he was without radio communication with his pit. He said he was able to tell his crew how his car was handling by punching either black or red buttons on his steering wheel.

"After our radios went down I had to tell them what the car was doing by hitting either the black or red button on my steering wheel," explained Unser. "One of the buttons told them it was loose, the other told them it was pushing. So at least I was able to tell them what the car was doing but

THE 1994 RACE

we weren't able to get the car as right as quick as we would have liked if the radio had been working."

Unser's second win at Indianapolis came on the day of his father's 55th birthday. Four-time winner Al Sr. retired from racing Indy cars just two weeks earlier of course. "I asked dad a few days ago what he wanted for a birthday present," said Jr. "And he said, 'Win the race.' Then when dad an I were riding around the track in the pace car after the race and I said, 'There's Emerson's marks on the wall,' And dad said, 'See it does come back to you at his place.'" Al Sr.'s reference was to the '89 Indy 500 when Fittipaldi and Al Jr. ran into each other in the second to last lap with Unser crashing and Fittipaldi winning.

Second place was taken by rookie Jacques Villeneuve who drove an outstanding race. The 23-year-old Villeneuve was the only other driver to run the full 200 laps, crossing the line 8.6 seconds behind Unser, under the yellow flag. Villeneuve was one of the few drivers to keep any pressure on the Penske-Mercedes cars. He was also the only driver other than Fittipaldi and Unser to lead any laps. Jacques twice led a handful of laps by running longer than the Penskes on a load of fuel.

"It feels fantastic," commented Villeneuve about his superb performance. "It's something that I never dreamed of - being on the podium. I was hoping to but I was never thinking I could make it. But I was very confident in the team. I knew they were capable of winning. I had to maintain my focus and do my job."

Villeneuve said his car didn't handle well as each fuel load was burned-off. "I had a lot of understeer at the beginning of the race and then after half-tanks it went to oversteer. It was getting sideways on me everywhere. That wasn't nice."

On his first pit stop, Villeneuve stalled his engine and lost eight positions.

300 MILES

Pos.	Car No.	Driver
1	2	Emerson Fittipaldi
2	31	Al Unser, Jr.
3	12	Jacques Villeneuve
4	18	Jimmy Vasser
5	9	Robby Gordon
6	4	Bobby Rahal
7	33	John Andretti
8	27	Eddie Cheever
9	8	Michael Andretti
10	11	Teo Fabi

A Penske gas man awaits an opportunity to refuel.

"I was really mad after that but it's a long race and the crew did a fantastic job on the pit stops. We also added some downforce during the pit stops and that made the car handle better. But I could never really push hard in traffic and it was very hard to pass in traffic.

"The important thing here is to remain focused and concentrated," added Villeneuve. "That's difficult to do when you're not pushing but that's what we had to do. I knew I couldn't beat the Penskes. Even though I was on the same lap as Al, I couldn't catch him. I just had to take it a little bit easy and bring it home." An excellent finish therefore, in Villeneuve's fourth Indy car race and first Indianapolis 500.

Third place ultimately went to Bobby Rahal who moved up a position after Michael Andretti was penalized a lap for ignoring a black flag passing a lapped car under a yellow. Rahal came from the tenth row aboard a leased '93 Penske-Ilmor after failing to qualify his Honda-powered Lola.

"It was a great day," said Rahal. "I got caught up in traffic and stuck behind the pace car a few times so that hurt us. We got caught in the wrong places. My pit stops were out of sync because during the first stop I stalled and that cost us. But the race was pretty good. I'm just happy to have finished, no less finish third. Two weeks ago we weren't even sure we would be in the race."

Top; Roger Penske watches as Emmo and Little Al battle for the lead. Bottom; Fittipaldi dominates, leading a whopping 145 laps.

THE 1994 RACE

400 MILES

Pos.	Car No.	Driver
1	2	Emerson Fittipaldi
2	31	Al Unser, Jr.
3	12	Jacques Villeneuve
4	9	Robby Gordon
5	4	Bobby Rahal
6	18	Jimmy Vasser
7	8	Michael Andretti
8	11	Teo Fabi
9	14	Bryan Herta
10	91	Stan Fox

Top; Nigel Mansell and Dennis Vitolo end up in a bizarre position. Bottom; Bobby Rahal salvaged his month with a third place finish.

Also impressing was Jimmy Vasser who ran with the leaders all the way and finished a strong fourth. Vasser lost ground halfway through the race when he had to make an extra stop under the green to remove a plastic bag that was blocking a radiator. He came back from thirteenth to finish fourth.

"We had a great run," commented Vasser. "We never had to change the car in the pits all day. I just played with the bars and if we hadn't had to make that extra stop we would have been even stronger."

Fifth place went to Robby Gordon who also had to make an extra pit stop. Gordon had to stop again after what should have been his last pit

103

THE 1994 RACE

500 MILES

Pos.	Car No.	Driver
1	31	Al Unser, Jr.
2	12	Jacques Villeneuve
3	4	Bobby Rahal
4	18	Jimmy Vasser
5	9	Robby Gordon
6	8	Michael Andretti
7	11	Teo Fabi
8	27	Eddie Cheever
9	14	Bryan Herta
10	33	John Andretti

stop. No fuel went into his car because the fuel valve on his pit side tank wasn't properly opened.

"We could have had third place," said Gordon. "I know we were quicker than Rahal because I had pulled him by twenty-two seconds on the last segment. But we finished. We brought it home. That's the third race in a row we've finished and that's what we're planning to keep on doing at each race."

Michael Andretti was a very disappointed

Left; Emmo self-destructs in turn #4, dashing his expectations of a third win. Right; Al Jr. ran easily to the checkered flag with Fittipaldi eliminated. Opposite; Emmo dealt with defeat.

sixth after running a strong third behind Fittipaldi and Unser through the race's early stages. Michael lost a lap when he cut a tire on debris from that early incident however. Even so he pulled his way back into the hunt and was running third at the end of the 500 only to be given a one-lap penalty by USAC. The penalty was given because observers said Andretti denied having done so although an appeal by team owner Chip Ganassi was rejected by race officials.

"That cut tire cost us almost two laps," said Andretti, "because we had to stop under the green. It got us out of sync with everyone else as well so

THE 1994 RACE

that we were running on full tanks when they were running on empty tanks. If we hadn't had that flat we would have finished second."

Notable non-finishers included Fittipaldi, Paul Tracy, Nigel Mansell, Mario Andretti and Raul Boesel. Tracy moved up well from the back of the field but dropped out just before half-distance with a blown turbocharger. PPG Cup champion Mansell was running a good third behind Fittipaldi and Unser when he was eliminated in a nasty-looking accident with Dennis Vitolo during a yellow. Vitolo didn't respond quickly enough to the yellow, lost control and spun into Mansell.

Vitolo's car came to a rest on top of Mansell's machine and Nigel was lucky to scramble to safety without any injuries other than a crimped neck

Opposite; Al Unser, Jr. and family celebrate in victory circle for the second time. Left; Little Al gives his dad the best birthday present ever.

and slight concussion. Earlier in the race Mansell was given a stop-and-go penalty for passing Raul Boesel in the pit lane under the yellow. Twenty laps passed between the questioned maneuver and the black flag penalty so that Mansell was already a very unhappy man, before Vitolo took him out of the race. Later, Mansell expressed his displeasure in no uncertain terms and as the year wore on it seemed unlikely that the Englishman will return again to race at Indianapolis.

And then there was front row starter Raul Boesel who was never a contender in the race. Boesel's engine began to lose water from the start and he finally retired from the race after 250 miles with a broken water pump.

The top ten finishers in the 78th 500 were completed by 1983's rookie of the year Teo Fabi in seventh place, Eddie Cheever in eighth and A.J. Foyt's drivers Bryan Herta and John Andretti in ninth and tenth. Herta was particularly impressive, moving up steadily and coming home ahead of his teammate despite stalling in the pits on one occasion. This was an excellent performance for a man in the very first Indy car race of his career and it appears that in Indy Lights champion Herta, Foyt has found himself a talented new driver.

Gordon Kirby is American Editor of the British weekly Autosport and Editor at Large of Racer magazine.

107

By Mark Robinson

Many thought he came from nowhere to finish a startling second as a rookie in the 1994 Indianapolis 500. But Jacques Villeneuve had been preparing for just such a shining moment much of his 23 years — even if those provisions were made in endeavors with what seemed little relation to open-wheel racing.

Racing, or any activity where pushing the envelope is the desired result, is as prevalent in Villeneuve's circulatory system as red blood cells. His father, Gilles, was an accomplished Formula One driver before his life was taken in a practice crash at the 1982 Belgian Grand Prix. Jacques' uncle and namesake drove the Indy-car circuit for several years in the 1980s, finishing 15th in his only Indy 500 appearance in '86.

But young Jacques' fancy wasn't necessarily to follow in his family's tire tracks. Instead, he took up such benign hobbies as cliff diving, ice hockey, motocross and skiing. In their own way, each peril helped groom Villeneuve for his achievement last May. But it's in downhill skiing where the fleet Canadian most readily sees the connection to his blossoming auto racing career.

"They're both hard sports where you have to be the fastest within the limits that other people set," says Villeneuve. "In slalom it will be tight gates, or a difficult downhill, or on a track like Indy, or a track like Long Beach. There is a limit that's set and you have to use it as much as possible to your own advantage.

"Then there's something mechanical between you and the ground — there's the

Jacques Villeneuve

car or there are the skis — which you have to control yourself, which you have to feel," he continues. "OK, skiing and driving a car is not the same. But the similarities are you need the coordination and you need to get in a mode where your body reacts to what it feels without you thinking. Everything becomes automatic.

"When you get to the top of slalom and are gonna go for the start, it's a little bit like the start of a race. You're all concentrated and you're almost in slow motion, then, bang, you have to go. It's like a new world. You see only the race track or the gates, and there's nothing else. You hear yourself breathing, you almost hear yourself talking to yourself. It's almost as if there's another person that tells you what to do sometimes."

It's just such an inner focus and resolve that permitted Villeneuve to become the top rookie finisher at Indianapolis since Roberto Guerrero was also runner-up in 1984. Villeneuve was able to shake the mental effects of crashes in two of his first three Indy-car races in '94 — including a much-maligned meeting with a stationary car at Phoenix — to climax a flawless month of May with a flawless performance on race day. Villeneuve was the top newcomer, in practice,

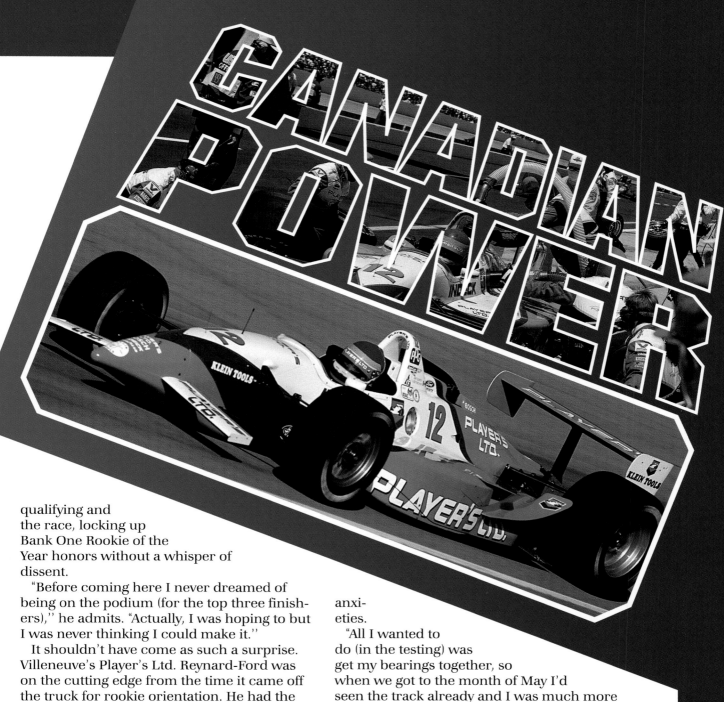

CANADIAN POWER

qualifying and the race, locking up Bank One Rookie of the Year honors without a whisper of dissent.

"Before coming here I never dreamed of being on the podium (for the top three finishers)," he admits. "Actually, I was hoping to but I was never thinking I could make it."

It shouldn't have come as such a surprise. Villeneuve's Player's Ltd. Reynard-Ford was on the cutting edge from the time it came off the truck for rookie orientation. He had the machine screaming past 226 miles an hour by the third day of practice for the "500." The car, driver and crew were so attuned that Villeneuve put in barely more than 250 laps of practice all month, less than half what a sizable number of other drivers turned.

Despite his youth and first meeting with a superspeedway, Villeneuve obviously was not intimidated by the hallowed Brickyard surroundings. Partaking in a pair of winter test sessions at the Speedway helped alleviate any anxieties.

"All I wanted to do (in the testing) was get my bearings together, so when we got to the month of May I'd seen the track already and I was much more relaxed," Villeneuve explains. Being quick early on put him even more at ease.

"From the start the car was great. It felt good so we could work on it. During the whole month we'd get it a touch better, a touch better every time.

"When you're at that speed and close to the edge, it's easy to go above it. The fine-tuning is very important because it means you can run closer to the edge without going above it. But when the set-up is not right, the edge is much

lower and it's much easier to go over.

"I had the benefit of being on a great team, people that had experience at Indianapolis. (Team manager and co-owner) Barry Green and the whole crew, and Tony Cicale as well, who's one of the best engineers. We had a good trust in each other, so we could work well together."

The Forsythe-Green team served notice when it set up a car that Villeneuve qualified on the inside of row 2 on the first day of time trials. His one-lap best (227.061 mph) and four-lap average (226.259) shattered the previous rookie records by nearly 4 mph each.

"I knew the laps were good for us, but I didn't know how good they were," Villeneuve says. "The team was ecstatic. It is always nice when you see your team with a big smile, with a big grin. Then there was the crowd as well cheering. It probably gave me a little taste of what (race day) was like."

Before he could truly experience race day, however, Villeneuve was due for two excruciatingly long weeks of waiting. To divert attention from the pressures at hand, the whole team went to Milwaukee for a couple days of testing in the middle of the second week of practice at Indy.

Jacques moments before his premiere at the Indianapolis 500.

"We wanted to get our minds off of Indianapolis," Villeneuve admits. "One of those things that can be a mistake is if you think only Indianapolis, then you can work differently than what you usually work. You need to take it as any other race.

"It's so much more important but it's good if you don't fall into that trap. You can make mistakes you wouldn't make normally. You get all pumped up and stressed out. When it comes to race day, with three weeks like that non-stop, something will go wrong."

Apparently, the diversionary tactic worked.

Nothing went wrong for Villeneuve on race day. The team had simple goals: "to not make mistakes and at least finish in the top 10." Mission accomplished — and then some — though Villeneuve admits to some trepidation when the race began.

"It was a crazy start," he recalls, his eyes widening. "There were cars everywhere. I didn't expect them to give the green flag. I just relaxed and I lifted (off the throttle) a little bit because I didn't want to be in my first Indy, in the first corner and in the middle of all the mish-mash, and do something stupid."

Starting fourth, Villeneuve slipped to eighth after one lap and was still holding that spot 20 laps later when Guerrero crashed. Villeneuve's only mistake of the day may have come on his first pit stop.

"Coming in I was following some back markers and they were going only 30 miles per hour down the pit road. I lost a lot of time there and then I stalled it as well. I pitted out and I was like 14th or 15th. I did not have a good feeling at that point."

Maybe, but a slight aerodynamic change during the stop put Villeneuve's Reynard in harmony with the track for the rest of the day. Though he set no land speed records — his fastest lap all day was 212.344 mph, a full 8 mph slower than the top circuit posted by Emerson Fittipaldi — Villeneuve plodded along at a consistent clip and continued to clip away the cars ahead of him.

"We just kept our pace and somehow gained positions," he says. "I didn't even know exactly who was in the position ahead of me. I just paid attention when there was a car in front of me — I didn't know if it was a lapped car or not — not to get too close to it going into the corners so I would have to slow down. Maybe slowing a little bit earlier, maintaining a good speed in the corners and maybe exit faster and get the tow and all that. It worked out we ended up making up a lot of positions."

Villeneuve was back in the top 10 by the 125-mile mark. By 150 miles, he was third — trailing only the Marlboro missiles guided by Al Unser Jr. and Fittipaldi. When the Penske cars pitted a lap apart, Villeneuve found himself in the most improbable of positions on lap 62: in first place.

"At the speed you come down the straight you don't really see your (pit) board that well," explains Villeneuve. "I saw '1' and I thought, 'Did they say pit in one lap?' The next time around I looked at the big pole with all the cars on it (the scoring pylon) and I saw my number at the top of it. I said, 'What? That's great!'

"I knew that was because the Penskes had come into their pits a few laps before us, but that was still a great feeling. I think that in a way that helped me remain focused and concentrated to the end of the race."

The Canadian flash led

Villeneuve kept up with the Penskes, leading seven laps of his own.

for two laps before Fittipaldi and then Unser roared back past. Villeneuve was well aware that his Ford engine was no match for the mighty Mercedes-Benz powering the Penskes, so he was content to ride it out where he was.

"I could see that the guys behind me weren't catching me so it was better to do it safe and sure than going crazy. The other factor was the two guys in front of me were the Penskes and I knew they were faster. There was no point taking any risks and keeping their pace

was taking a big risk."

A conservative approach? Maybe, but it also contributed to Villeneuve getting back on the lead lap after Fittipaldi had put him one down on lap 74.

"A lot of times when I was blocked in traffic and I couldn't take them, I would just lift a little and take the tow. I think we managed to save fuel like that."

Which allowed Villeneuve more laps between stops, and eventually, one less stop than the other front-runners.

When Fittipaldi had to pit for fuel under green on lap 90, Villeneuve stayed out and unlapped himself. Two laps later Hideshi Matsuda spun into the turn 1 wall, bringing out the fourth caution period of the race. Pitting under yellow, Villeneuve was able to remain with Fittipaldi and Unser on the lead lap.

Driving beyond his years, the youngest starter in the '94 race wasn't about to abandon the sure-footed approach that had carried him this far. By the same token, he knew he also could not let up mentally. One false move at these searing speeds, and the ingredients for a memorable day would go into the trash with so many shattered pieces of his car.

"A lot of guys that were behind me were a lap down on the leaders, if not to me," he remembers. "We had quite a bit advance on them so at that point all I wanted to do was not make mistakes."

That's not to say there weren't a few anxious moments.

"There's a few times where, when you're in a corner, you just lose the front grip or lose the rear. It happens so quickly. And there were a few times when I was going straight for the wall and I do not know why I did not hit it. It was just a matter of an inch or something."

Villeneuve led laps 125-129, again after the Penske cars came into the pits for fuel and tires. The seven total laps he headed the field were the only circuits not paced by a Penske all day.

Despite the admitted inferiority of his car, Villeneuve remained on the lead lap until the dominating Fittipaldi overtook the Player's Reynard on lap 157.

As the waning laps began to trickle away, and Fittipaldi and Unser pulled further away, Villeneuve had all but accepted a third-place finish. Until the improbable occurred.

Fittipaldi, blazing toward his second straight Indianapolis win and having just passed Unser to put the entire field a lap behind, lost the back end of his Penske-Mercedes coming out of turn 4 on lap 185 and smacked the wall. Unser inherited the lead from his teammate, with Villeneuve on the same lap.

When the green flag re-emerged on lap 190, Unser and Villeneuve were separated by five seconds and 13 back markers. Racing instinct was tugging down on Villeneuve's right foot, itching him to make a charge through the field. Reason won out. Knowing the only way he would take first place would be for Unser

to make a mistake — an unlikely scenario — Villeneuve concentrated solely on not making one of his own.

"When we were running second at the end, I knew we had had a great day," he says with pride. "I just didn't want to see that great day end by making a stupid mistake. ... It would have been stupid to pull the knives out and risk it all."

While Villeneuve played it cool, Unser's advantage stretched to as much as 33 seconds before Stan Fox's crash brought out the last caution on lap 197. The checkered and yellow flags were waved simultaneously as Unser crept across the finish line 8.6 second ahead of Villeneuve.

"I was relieved when I saw the start-finish line (on the last lap)," Villeneuve admits.

Relieved, and most assuredly not disappointed. He and Unser were the only drivers to complete all 200 laps. He'd outdriven all but one. Some of the greatest drivers in the world — Bobby Rahal, Michael and Mario Andretti, Nigel Mansell and Fittipaldi among them — were looking up to this boyish hot-foot on the leader board.

Jacques was the center of attention after his phenomenal second place finish.

Circling the Speedway one last time after taking the checkered was a time to embrace what was, not what might have been.

"I was already in second in the team's first year at Indy, in my first season as well. It was already unbelievable, so there was no frustration. Winning would have been great, but maybe it would have been too much."

Could be. For, on this day, Jacques Villeneuve had already accomplished plenty.

PPG Pole Award - $100,000
PPG INDUSTRIES
Plus a 1994 customized Starcraft /Ford van ($35,000 value)
STARCRAFT CORPORATION and FORD MOTOR COMPANY
Al Unser, Jr.

GTE "Front Runner" Award - $30,000
$10,000 awarded to each front row driver
GTE NORTH, INC.
Al Unser, Jr., Raul Boesel, Emerson Fittipaldi

Starcraft "Pole Position Car Owner" Award - $10,000
STARCRAFT AUTOMOTIVE CORPORATION
Roger Penske

True Value "Master Mechanic" Award - $10,000
plus Lawn Chief Garden Tractor awarded to pole position chief mechanic
COTTER AND COMPANY
Richard Buck

D.L. Clark Candy "Slo-Poke" Award - $10,000
slowest official qualifier
D.L. CLARK CANDY
Bryan Herta

Sure Start/Automotive Armature "On The Bubble" Award - $10,000
awarded to the 33rd fastest qualifier
EXIDE CORPORATION
Bryan Herta

Ameritech Pages Plus® "Youngest Starting Driver" Award - $5,000
AMERITECH
Jacques Villeneuve

Ameritech "First in the Field" Award - $5,000
AMERITECH
Hideshi Matsuda

NewsPager "Most Consistent Qualifying Laps" Award - $5,000
NEWSPAGER CORPORATION OF AMERICA
Lyn St. James

S R E Industries "My Bubble Burst" Award - $5,000
awarded to the last driver to be bumped on last day of qualifying
SRE INDUSTRIES
Scott Goodyear

T.P. Donovan "Top Starting Rookie" Award - $5,000
OLINGER DISTRIBUTING COMPANY, INC.
Jacques Villeneuve

KLF/Race Spec "Final Measure" Award - $5,000
awarded to last team to pass inspection and qualify for the race
KLF/RACE SPEC
John Paul, Jr.

HotShots "Hottest Rookie Lap" Award - $5,000
awarded to the rookie posting the fastest qualifying lap
HOTSHOTS PHOTOGRAFX
Jacques Villeneuve

Raybestos/CAM "Tough Brakes" Award - $5,000
awarded to the crew which displays persistance despite great adversity during qualifying
RAYBESTOS/CHAMPIONSHIP ASSOCIATION OF MECHANICS, INC.
Scott Goodyear

Snap-On/CAM "500 Top Wrench" Award - $5,000
awarded to the chief mechanic demonstrating outstanding skill and expertise during qualifying
SNAP-ON/CHAMPIONSHIP ASSOCIATION OF MECHANICS, INC.
John Paul, Jr.

1-800-COLLECT "MOST IMPROVED POSITION" AWARD
$10,000 - 1-800-COLLECT
Bobby Rahal

AMERICAN DAIRY AWARDS
$12,500 - American Dairy Association
(winner, fastest rookie, winning chief mechanic)
Al Unser, Jr., Jacques Villeneuve, Richard Buck

**BANK ONE, INDIANAPOLIS
"ROOKIE OF THE YEAR" AWARD**
$10,000 - Bank One, Indianapolis
Jacques Villeneuve

BORG-WARNER TROPHY AWARD
$100,000 plus trophy replica - Borg-Warner Automotive, Inc.
(race winner)
Al Unser, Jr.

CHAPMAN S. ROOT AWARD
$5,000 - Terre Haute First National Bank
(race leader at lap 48)
Emerson Fittipaldi

**CLINT BRAWNER
MECHANICAL EXCELLENCE AWARD**
$5,000 - Clint Brawner Mechanical Excellence
Award Foundation
Craig Baranouski

RICHARD DEERING CLEANERS "WORKHORSE" AWARD
$5,000 - Richard Deering Cleaners, Inc.
*(awarded to the driver who records the
most practice laps during May)*
Emerson Fittipaldi

DowElanco MILESTONE AWARDS
$25,000 - DowElanco
(race leaders at 100, 200, 300 and 400 miles)
Emerson Fittipaldi

EARLY WINE "36TH ANNIVERSARY" AWARD
$5,000 - J.T. Earlywine & Associates
(race leader at lap 36)
Emerson Fittipaldi

FORD OFFICIAL PACE CAR AWARD
1994 Ford Mustang Pace Car
Ford Motor Company
Al Unser, Jr.

GOODYEAR "WINNING CAR OWNER" AWARD
$5,000 plus ring - The Goodyear Tire and Rubber Co.
Roger Penske

HERFF JONES "CHAMPION OF CHAMPIONS" AWARD
$15,000 plus winner's ring - Herff Jones, Inc.
(race winner)
Al Unser, Jr.

IBM "FASTEST LAP" AWARD
$10,000 - IBM Corporation
(fastest single lap of the race)
Emerson Fittipaldi

INDIANA GAS "ON THE GAS" AWARD
$5,000 - Indiana Gas Company, Inc.
(awarded to the leader at lap 4)
Al Unser, Jr.

INDIANA OXYGEN "PERSEVERANCE" AWARD
$5,000 - Indiana Oxygen
Eddie Cheever

JCPENNEY "500" WINNER QUILT AWARD
$5,000 and quilt by Jeanetta Holder - JCPenney Co. Inc.
Al Unser, Jr.

KLIPSCH SPEAKERS "EFFICIENCY" AWARD
$5,000 - Klipsch Speakers
*(awarded to the team that runs the most miles
between pit stops)*
Raul Boesel - Dick Simon Racing

KODAK "PHOTO FINISH" AWARD
$7,500 - Eastman Kodak Company
(race winner)
Al Unser, Jr.

LOCTITE AWARDS
$10,500 - Loctite Corporation and Permatex Fast Orange
(winner, winning chief mechanic, pole position)
Al Unser, Jr., Richard Buck, Al Unser, Jr.

MBNA "CHAMPIONSHIP DRIVERS" MASTERCARD AWARD
$55,000 - MBNA
*(divided among top five finishers who wear the
Championship Drivers Group patch during May)*
*Bobby Rahal, Jimmy Vasser, Michael Andretti,
Eddie Cheever, Brian Till*

MARLBORO "500 MILE CLUB" AWARD
$75,000 - Philip Morris U.S.A.
(divided among drivers competing 500 miles)
Al Unser, Jr., Jacques Villeneuve

MARSH "LEADER AT LAP 5" AWARD
$5,000 - Marsh Supermarkets, Inc.
*(race leader at lap 5 - honoring Marsh5-A-Day Program
teaching children the importance of nutrition)*
Al Unser, Jr.

MILLER INDY PIT STOP CHAMPIONSHIP
$51,000 - Miller Brewing Company
(contest held May 26, 1994)
Jacques Villeneuve

MOLEX "HARD CHARGER" AWARD
$5,000 plus plaque - Molex
Bringing people and technology together, worldwide
(awarded to the lowest qualifier to lead the race)
Jacques Villeneuve

**MOTORSPORTS SPARES/GOODRIDGE
"PERSISTENCE PAYS" AWARD**
$5,000 - Motorsports Spares Int'l Inc./Goodridge
(awarded to the highest finishing last day qualifier)
Marco Greco

NBD "LEADERS' CIRCLE" AWARD
$10,000 - NBD Bank
(awarded to the driver who leads the most laps in the race)
Emerson Fittipaldi

NATIONAL CITY BANK "CHECKERED FLAG" AWARD
$10,000 - National City Bank, Indiana
(race winner)
Al Unser, Jr.

SEARS CRAFTSMAN "FASTEST PIT CREW" AWARD
$30,000 - Sears, Roebuck & Co.
(least accumulative time in the pits)
Jacques Villeneuve

115

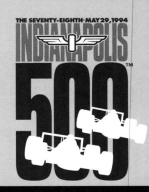
BELL HELMETS
$6,000

ROBERT BOSCH CORPORATION
$45,000

BOWES SEAL FAST CORPORATION
$10,000

CANON, U.S.A
$7,500

CHAMPION SPARK PLUG
$60,000

DELCO REMY, GMC
$15,500

EARL'S PERFORMANCE PRODUCTS
$13,500

EMCO GEARS, INC.
$5,000

FIRST BRANDS - STP RACING
$24,000

HYPERCO INC.
$5,000

ILMOR ENGINEERING
$5,000

IDEAL DIVISION/STANT CORP.
$5,000

INTERSTATE BATTERY SYSTEM
$5,000

LOCTITE CORPORATION
$9,500

MALLORY INC.
$5,000

MOBIL OIL CORPORATION
$30,000

MONROE AUTO EQUIPMENT
$20,000

PPG INDUSTRIES, INC.
$396,000

PENNZOIL PRODUCTS COMPANY
$5,000

PREMIER INDUSTRIAL CORPORATION
$10,000

QUAKER STATE CORPORATION
$5,000

RAYBESTOS/BRAKE PARTS INC.
$20,000

SEARS CRAFTSMAN TRACTORS
$5,000

SEARS DIEHARD BATTERY
$14,500

SIMPSON RACE PRODUCTS
$5,000

SNAP-ON TOOLS CORP.
$5,000

STANT MANUFACTURING, INC.
$5,000

TEXACO LUBRICANTS COMPANY
$5,000

VALVOLINE, INC.
$35,000

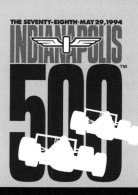

USAC OFFICERS

Robert G. Moorhead, Chairman of the Board; **Richard King,** President; **Johnny Capels,** Vice President/Competition Director; **Robert Cassaday,** Vice President/Administration; **Michael Devin,** Vice President/Technical Director; **Art Graham,** Vice President/Development; **Bill Marvel,** Vice President/Director of Corporate Affairs; **Gary Sokola,** Deputy Competition Director; **Tommy Hunt,** Vice President; **Dick Jordan,** Communications Director; **Donald Davidson,** Statistician/Historian; **Ron Green,** Communications.

EXECUTIVE OFFICIALS

Thomas W. Binford, Chief Steward; Arthur D. Meyers, Senior Steward; Robert Cassaday, Steward/Chief Registrar; Keith Ward, Steward; Rich Coy, Steward/Chairman of Product Certification; Duane Sweeney, Chief Starter; Ray Chaike - Bill Carey, Assistant Starters;

USAC TECHNICAL OPERATIONS

Michael Devin, Technical Director; Jack Beckley, Donald McGregor, Technical Advisors; Jerry Grobe, Deputy Director; Dennis Hunley, Deputy Director NDT & Metallurgical Committee; D.Ray Marshall, Deputy Director, Race-Spec; Samuel Burge, Richard Gunder, Ray Linton, Mike Smith and William Sparks, Supervisors; Andy Anderson, Anne Grobe, J.W. Grobe, Jack Jenkins, Roam Jordan, Steve Jordan, David Kyle, Ben Lawrence, Ray Macht, Pat Martin, Mike Muller, Marcel Periat, Ron Scudder, Russ Stone, Terry Taylor, William Teeguarden, Jeff VanTreese and Jon VanTreese, Vice Chairmen; Don McGregor, Advisor.

USAC TECHNICAL ASSISTANTS

Dennis Brankle, Gary Brewer, Lila Brewer, Jeff Collins, Bud Edwards, Rick Hoy, Joseph Mackell, Nancy Marshall, Tom Miller, Rick Myers, Kevin Park, Paul Park, Sandy Park, Steve Park, Paul Powers, Mike Reffitt, John Shark, Dave Simpson, Larry Stubbs, Dennis Thacker, Race Spec Inspection; E.Budy, Jr., B.Collins, J.Freeze, J.Hunley, S.Hunley, C.Kiracofe, J.Knavel, S. Kontney, T.L. Kontney, C.Majors, M.McLaughlin, B.Messer, G.Monks, H.Rohm, Jr., C.Small, L.Snyder, W.Tarpley, D.Taylor and C.Trotter, Non-Destructive Testing; Dave King, Communications; Harry Robertson, Fuel Cell Advisor; Ray Carpenter and Terry Haley, Assistant Weigh Masters; Pat McCarty, Vicky Ray, Martha Shields and Toni Sylvester, Technical Data; A.Adastik, A.Albrecht, D.Anderson, A.Ankerman, P.Asa, H.Baker, J.Baker, Rodney Banks, D.Barrett, S.Bell, A.Biggs, R.Bivens, G.Bloeser, J.Bornhorst, W.Brizius, F.Burdette, R.Butterfield, P.Cannaley, R.Carson, J.Clark, V.Clossin, B.Clough, F.Collins, J.Cowley, D.Cox, E.Cox, C.Curry, W.Dunkerson, D.Dunning, A.Edgar, K.Edwards, M.Ehnert, R.Elsner, B.Fahey, C.Fielder, C.Fischer, W.Frame, G.Frashier, J.Fullan, J.M.Grobe, R.Grobe, R.Hanson, C.Harmon, C.Hartzer, L.Hawkins, E.Held, D.Herling, W.Hittenberger, J.Innis, J.Jenkins, J.Johnson, J.Keith, W.Koleta, K.Krimmel, S.Lewis, B.Lockwood, D.Love, G.Maerki, J.Maher, T.Martin, J.Mastin, J.Mayhew, H.Merritt, M.Milharcik, J.Muller, R.Murphy, R.Nicoloff, J.Nims, C.Parmelli, S.Pelsor, A.Pickett, M.Ray, J. Rayhel, D.Riffel, B.Runyon, M.Sandler, A.Schmidt, M.Selode, N.Shields, B.Smith, J.Smith, K.Smith, F.Snow, F.Stewart, W.Strong, B.Turner, R.VanNote, D.Verrill, A.Vesely, W.Wacker, C.Wasdyke, T.Westell, R.White, P.Wilson, G.Yohe, Technical Observers.

USAC CERTIFICATION COMMITTEE

Rich Coy, Chairman, Product Certification; William Conley, Deputy Director; Frank Wilhelm, Deputy Director; D.Cherry, C.Colip, R.Condit, S.Ingle, A.Johnson, M.Judy, D.Kischell, W.Kuhn, S.Lanham, J.Locke, G.Mayfield, D.Nicely, J.Proper, D.Smith, T.Vastine, Vice Chairmen.

USAC SAFETY OFFICIALS

Jack Gilmore, Director; Robert Nolen, Deputy Director.

MISCELLANEOUS

Supervisor of Track Fire Prevention - Jack Gilmore; Score Board Manager - David Adams; Chief Announcer - Tom Carnegie; Telephone Service - Indiana Bell Co. and AT&T; Wrecker Service - No*Mar Towing Equipment; Wheel Aligning and Balancing Service - Bear; and Welding Service - Indiana Oxygen Company.

USAC TIMING & SCORING OFFICIALS

Art Graham, Director: Les Kimbrell, Director of Scoring Operations; Larry Allen, Chief Scoring Technician; Jerry L. Challis, Chief Scorer; Dennis Dyer, Chief Scoring Engineer; Andrew Graham, Chief of Scoring Systems; Harold Hamilton, Chief Timing Engineer; Kay Kimbrell, Chief Serial Scorer; Jack Taylor, Chief Scoring Observer; George Vogelsperger, Chief Pit Scorer; Dick Webb, Chief Auditor; Chuck Whetsel, Chief Scoring Judge; Bert Wilkerson, Chief of Scoring Equipment; Mike Cramer, Chief Scoring Registrar; Ray House, Chief Timer Emeritus; Bob Lohman, Honorary Chief Scorer; Tony Fascenda, Honorary Scoring Engineer;
TIMING & SCORING STAFF: Bill Ballard Jr., Dave Berryman, Andy Blahut, Bob Blahut, Byron Bolton, Barbara Bucher, Dan Challis, Bob Cole, Susie Ebershoff Coles, Joyce Diemer, Patrick Diemer, Linda Foster, Veronica Frost, Norm Funkhouser, D.J. Garrison, Michael Gray, Bob Hicks, Ryan Hoover, Lisa Lengerich, Ed Long, Larry Martin, Dawn Moss, Craig Newman, Gary Paschke, Larry Potter, Kent Rebman, Nick Reed, Bill Reeser, Dale Smiley, Bill Spellerberg, Bill Stevens, Don Stone, Craig Wambold, Bert Wilkerson II, Terry Wilkerson, Chuck Yoder, Lenny Zwik. TECHNICAL PARTNERS STAFF: Mike Day, Carol Callan, Ed Logan, Tom Murphy (IBM Corp.); Scooter Willis, Kent Tambling (GDS Engineering); Ray Szeluga (Lexmark Corp.).
   ADDITIONAL RACE DAY PERSONNEL: J. Akers, L. Albean, M. Albean, B. Alexander, B. Armbruster, L. Ashburn, J. Baden, J. Ballard+III, J. Bertholf, C. Blackwell IV, S. Blank, C. Brethman, R. Bromwell, B. Campbell, D. Campbell, B. Chasteen, W. Coles, L. Crane, S. Crane, S. Demeter, M. Ellis, R. Fegan, D. Fisher, B. Gardner, J. Garrett, D. Graham, S. Gray, S. Griffith, R. Hanes, G. Harabin, L. Harabin, R. Harvey, N. Hastings, S. Holt Jr., Randy Hoover, S. Hoover, B. Hunter, D. Hunter, S. Hunter, P. Karle, R. Kenyon, J. Lane, E. Leduke, B. Lindholm, J. Lynch, C. Macomber, T. McKinney, L. Mitchell, B. Mooney, B. Moore, H. Moore, S. Moore, C. Moorman, J. Morphy, B. Mount, B. Moyer, A. Neuner, S. Oliver, L. Olson, J. Paschke, K. Paschke, Jeff Perkins, Jim Perkins, John Perkins, J. Pingle, J. Reed, D. Renzoni, R. Renzoni, B. Reynolds, D. Richey, E. Rodman, D. Rutledge, C. Schendel, J. Schuh, M. Sedam, C. Serafin, S. Steele, R. Stone, Jeff Taylor, C. Tunny, L. Vastine, Greg Vogelsperger, P. Voorhees, S. Voorhees, B. Weir, D. Wilkerson, T. Worthington, S. Wright, J. Youngblood. **Trackside Computing by the IBM PS/2 with OS/2, the Information Systems Choice of the United States Auto Club Data Processing Services courtesy of IBM INDIANA.**

USAC OBSERVERS

Claude Fisher, Chief Observer; Edwin Board, Ted Lake, John Notte III and Robert Stanley, Deputy Chief Observers; Dennis Barker, Jim Best, Jeff Boles, Butch Bundrant, Richard Eiler, Gary Goodrich, Richard Hoehnke, Pat Johnson, Mike Lake, Jim Nell III and Glenn Timmis, Assistant Chief Observers.

OBSERVERS

S.Amos, J.Bailey, A.Barker, R.J.Barron, R.N.Barron, D.Barth, M.Bennett, N.Bennett, R.Bentley, R.Best, T.Blanchard, W.Borecki, J.Boucher, J.Brasker, R.Brown, G.Bundrant, J.Butler, R.Clark, M.L. Coble, M.Cox, R.Cox, Jr., S.Cox, D.Crouch, L.Davis, V.Dentice, D.Distler, J.Dudley, G.Edwards, L.Ellis, D.Emerick, E.Florian, D.Fox, F.Frost, D.Goonen, R.Hamilton, J.Hanna, J.Haynes, J.Highsmith, R.Hogan, L.Hough, G.Humphrey, C.Hurt, L.Hurt, K.Kruty, L.Kunkle, F.Kurtz, D.Lanham, S.Lawson, N.Lebamoff, R.Ledbetter, L.Leser, W.Ligocki, D.Lindsey, W.Loucks, R.Maas, P.Manuel, T.Martin, B.Miller, G.Motsinger, P.Panhorst, G.Parsons, D.Price, J.Randolph, R.Rude, K.Ruddick, J.Schaffner, R.Schroeder, G.Schultz, Scott Schultz, Steve Schultz, B.Sewell, J.Simko, G.Snider, J.Snider, T.Stawicki, C.Steele, R.Stoddard, G.Sweeney, M.Sweeney, R.Tharp, D.Thompson, M.Thompson, N.Trebing, D.Trice, G.Tushar, R.Vannice, J.Walden, G.Werner, S.West, P.Whalen, G.Wirey, E.Wright, P.J. Wyn, T.Wyn, Observers.

CHAPLAINS

Rev. Michael Welch and Dr. Andrew Crowley.

MEDICAL STAFF & SUPPORT

Administrative Staff: Medical Administrator, Cheryl Rumer, R.N.; Bruce B. Cross, Robert C. Held; Executive Secretary, Mary Simpson; Nursing Director, Terri Cordell, R.N.; Emergency Medial Services Coordinator, Andrew Bowes; Optometrist, E. Jerome Babitz, O.D.; Medical Director, Henry Bock, M.D.; Assistant Medical Director, Michael Olinger, M.D.; Laboratory and Cardiology Consultants: Methodist Hospital; Emergency Helicopter Service - American Eurocopter, Methodist LifeLine, H.H. Gregg; Medical Electronics: Hewlett Packard, IVAC, Laerdal, Welch Allyn.

1994 DAILY PRACTICE LAPS

CAR	DRIVER	YR/CH/E	5/07	5/08	5/09	5/10	5/11	5/12	5/13	5/14	5/15	5/16	5/17	5/18	5/19	5/20	5/21	5/22	5/26	TOTAL
1	Bryan Herta	94/L/F																	9	9
1	Nigel Mansell	94/L/F			33	87	44	98	66	29									27	384
1T	Nigel Mansell	94/L/F					20							57	53					130
2	Emerson Fittipaldi	94/P/MB		24	76	58	12	95	68	14	30						23		16	416
2T	Emerson Fittipaldi	94/P/MB											5							5
2T	Paul Tracy	94/P/MB											36		25		19			80
2T	Al Unser, Jr.	94/P/MB												107	101	52	19			279
3	Paul Tracy	94/P/MB		42	25	65	29	54	52											267
3T	Emerson Fittipaldi	94/P/MB										86	92	97	62		59	43		439
3T	Paul Tracy	94/P/MB		19	13											75				107
3T	Al Unser, Jr.	94/P/MB									22					21		44		87
4	Bobby Rahal	94/L/H		55	51	81	31	101	83	33										435
4T	Bobby Rahal	94/L/F		19	9															28
5	Raul Boesel	94/L/F		47	48	58		32	91	19		29	47	45				10	8	434
5T	Marco Greco	94/L/F						82												82
5T	Stephan Gregoire	94/L/F													46	14		22		82
5T	Buddy Lazier	94/L/F																27		27
5T	Tero Palmroth	94/L/F		20																20
5T	Dennis Vitolo	94/L/F				79	59													138
6	Mario Andretti	94/L/F		40	52	22	51	42	63	19	28		7						19	343
6T	Mario Andretti	94/L/F								21	24			86	83	30				244
7	Adrian Fernandez	94/R/IL		79	15	85	82		42				61						24	388
7T	Adrian Fernandez	94/R/IL		5	39								51	77	57	29				303
8	Michael Andretti	94/R/F			25	18	30		34	21		22	69							218
8T	Michael Andretti	94/R/F		38	36	48	3	21	18			56	25	34	16	18				327
9	Robby Gordon	94/L/F		82		72	45	41	58	26	24							30	23	400
9	Willy T. Ribbs	94/L/F																5		5
9	Mark Smith	94/L/F										12	3							15
9T	Robby Gordon	94/L/F			71		42	20									60			201
10	Mike Groff	94/L/H			46							49								95
10T	Mike Groff	94/L/H		83		17		74	86		35							12		318
11	Teo Fabi	94/R/IL			48	52	58	84	70	25	30		15	78	48					501
11T	Teo Fabi	94/R/IL		61	8	11				10			57							228
12	Jacques Villeneuve	94/R/F			90	68	5	84	34	29		59	57				30			535
12T	Jacques Villeneuve	94/R/F							18	15	24					4				39
14	Bryan Herta	94/L/F			6	21		64	80	26		29			75	18				377
14T	Bryan Herta	94/L/F			32							17								49
14T	Johnny Rutherford	94/L/F															2			2
15	Robby Gordon	94/L/F										25								25
15	Mark Smith	94/L/F			4	56	34	53	50	26	35	23	44		49	34			11	430
15T	Mark Smith	94/L/F			48	48											60			156
16	Stefan Johansson	93/P/IL			42	29	25	35	41	22	49			20	11	14		21	22	339
16T	Gary Bettenhausen	93/P/IL					5	19												27
16T	Stefan Johansson	93/P/IL								27	25									52
17	Dominic Dobson	94/L/F		75	85	53	46	50	48	25			25	74	75	4			23	583
18	Jimmy Vasser	94/R/F		6	58	76	22	42	28	15	24						44	6	16	337
18T	Jimmy Vasser	94/R/F						18	12				63		23	12				128
19	Brian Till	93/L/F		108	73	77	56	103	59	37						37	42	70	23	685
21	Roberto Guerrero	92/L/B		48	41	29	20	59	49	21									9	276
21T	Roberto Guerrero	92/L/B											24	11	46	37	4	41		152
22	Raul Boesel	94/L/F					19		18					11						48
22	Hiro Matsushita	94/L/F		64	35	17	37	35	61	28		43	30	13	26				16	397
23	Buddy Lazier	93/L/IL		66	6	20	51	62	46	10	45				73	41	52	49	20	565
23	Robby Gordon	93/L/IL							13			19								32
24	Willy T. Ribbs	94/L/F								32			21							
24	Willy T. Ribbs	94/L/F				45	5	56	75					15	48	48	48	24	48	377

1994 DAILY PRACTICE LAPS

CAR	DRIVER	YR/CH/E	5/07	5/08	5/09	5/10	5/11	5/12	5/13	5/14	5/15	5/16	5/17	5/18	5/19	5/20	5/21	5/22	5/26	TOTAL
24T	Willy T. Ribbs	93/L/F			37														31	68
25	Marco Greco	94/L/F		40	40				100	15	31				55	30		14		325
25T	Marco Greco	93/L/F														31	38	44	14	127
27	Eddie Cheever	93/L/M		41	33	68		75	44	27								10	21	319
27T	Scott Brayton	93/L/M									40							9	21	70
27T	Eddie Cheever	93/L/M			16		28			19										63
28	Arie Luyendyk	94/L/IL		43	46	44				24									28	198
28T	Arie Luyendyk	94/L/IL					29	80	37				25	74	24					310
30	Pancho Carter	93/L/IL		8					11	6										35
30	Stephan Gregoire	93/L/IL																47		47
30T	Pancho Carter	93/L/IL				45	35	47	71	10	21	7	48	58	43					385
31	Paul Tracy	94/P/MB		10																10
31	Al Unser, Jr.	94/P/MB			44	45	57	48	47	23							31		21	316
31T	Emerson Fittipaldi	94/P/MB					20													20
31T	Paul Tracy	94/P/MB									31				26				20	77
31T	Al Unser, Jr.	94/P/MB				13			12											25
33	John Andretti	94/L/F			28	60	26	46	12	7					9				15	228
39	Ross Bentley	93/L/F		59																59
40	Scott Goodyear	94/L/F		82	42	54	53	79	87	27			35	51	47	52	39	64		712
40T	Scott Goodyear	94/L/F			20					20	58								14	112
40T	Davy Jones	94/L/F													36	17	24			77
41T	Bryan Herta	93/L/F													6	62		84		152
42	Johnny Parsons	93/L/G		12					5	14	13									114
44	Roberto Moreno	94/L/F											43	66						109
44	Tero Palmroth	94/L/F													40	50	36	58		184
44	Al Unser	94/L/F			6	53	44	30	44	24	19									220
44T	Al Unser	93/L/F		21	21															42
45	John Paul, Jr.	93/L/IL		85	58	35	12	97	59	29	66				24	17	22		12	516
46	John Paul, Jr.	93/L/IL												73	19	23	28			143
50	Bobby Rahal	93P/IL												19	30	47	35			131
51	Eddie Cheever	92/L/M					18													18
52T	Mike Groff	93/P/IL												33	62	25	27		21	168
52T	Bobby Rahal	93/P/IL											32	20						52
52T	Paul Tracy	93/P/IL											10							10
59	Geoff Brabham	93/L/M												1	53		35			89
59	Scott Brayton	93/L/M		49		38	14	52	49	20	26		7	41		55				351
59T	Geoff Brabham	93/L/M															40	44		84
59T	Scott Brayton	93/L/M			34	21				27										82
59T	Eddie Cheever	93/L/M											29	39	26	59				153
61	Gary Bettenhausen	93/p/IL				14	40	39	39	18					40	47	12	32		281
64	Didier Theys	94/L/F														50	49	79		178
71	Dominic Dobson	94/L/F																4		4
71	Scott Sharp	94/L/F		64	95	56	46	65	47	31									19	423
71T	Dominic Dobson	94/L/F														31				31
71T	Scott Sharp	94/L/F											19	86	62		12		17	196
74	Jim Crawford	91/L/B		5	15	30	29	16	35			37	45		62	35	33			342
79	Dennis Vitolo	91/L/F		43	17			50	99	31							19		23	282
88	Mauricio Gugelmin	94/R/F		61	13	55	28	37	64	24										282
89	Mauricio Gugelmin	94/R/F												67	53	14	29		12	175
90	Lyn St. James	94/L/F		31	26	44	30	49	40	16			18	32	37				12	353
91	Stan Fox	94/R/F							42				28		37				7	113
94	Jeff Andretti	92/L/B												20	48	30	56	36		190
94	Stan Fox	92/L/B																		85
94	Buddy Lazier	92/L/B																14		14
95	Stan Fox	92/L/B			24															24
99	Hideshi Matsuda	93/L/F		50	32			40	51	22		13	24					22		254

1994 DAILY BEST SPEEDS

Car	Driver	YR/CH/E	5/07	5/08	5/09	5/10	5/11	5/12	5/13	5/14	5/15	5/16	5/17	5/18	5/19	5/20	5/21	5/22	5/26
1	Bryan Herta	94/L/F															188.198		
1	Nigel Mansell	94.L.F			220.978	227.969	225.807	226.609	226.895	228.137									222.552
1T	Nigel Mansell	94/L/F					222.398							221.697	223.508		225.034		222.872
2	Emerson Fittipaldi	94/P/MB		217.918	226.512	229.264	223.403	230.438	230.138	229.043	228.224								
2T	Emerson Fittipaldi	94/P/MB											224.025						
2T	Paul Tracy	94/P/MB										225.135		225.017		217.981			
2T	Al Unser, Jr.	94/P/MB												224.944	225.694	225.028			
3	Paul Tracy	94/P/MB		220.103	221.899	229.961	224.433	228.444	228.693										
3T	Emerson Fittipaldi	94/P/MB										226.421	228.717	229.510	228.305	219.802	223.043	219.550	
3T	Paul Tracy	94/P/MB		212.691	216.925											220.173		218.877	
3T	Al Unser, Jr.	94/P/MB									226.324					225.017			
4	Bobby Rahal	94/L/H		219.791	217.976	220.994	215.430	221.114	219.786	220.302									
4T	Bobby Rahal	94/L/H		213.802	212.104		217.854												
5	Raul Boesel	94/L/F		223.908	225.853	230.403		227.175	226.074	228.862		218.071	223.242	223.214				206.091	211.705
5T	Marco Greco	94/L/F						209.927											
5T	Stephan Gregoire	94/L/F														194.028	213.706	214.720	
5T	Buddy Lazier	94/L/F																212.485	
5T	Tero Palmroth	94/L/F		199.933															
5T	Dennis Vitolo	94/L/F				219.448	212.475												
6	Mario Andretti	94/L/F		223.753	224.629	228.351	225.519	225.705	227.618	228.606	225.615		222.794	224.557	224.266				223.708
6T	Mario Andretti	94/L/F																	217.765
7	Adrian Fernandez	94/R/IL		207.001	209.522	218.733	218.134	222.283	224.629	223.875	222.949								
7T	Adrian Fernandez	94/R/IL		222.761	215.864	226.723	224.949	226.986	226.330	228.600			218.537	216.258	215.182				
8	Michael Andretti	94/R/F		223.769	227.038	228.189		227.698	227.589	227.871		219.053	224.221	221.282				222.916	
8T	Michael Andretti	94/R/F			226.080	225.129		226.946	226.563	227.739		224.781	225.564	224.910				212.206	
9	Robby Gordon	94/L/F			196.412	217.113													
9	Willy T. Ribbs	94/L/F																	
9	Mark Smith	94/L/F			220.318			221.926	158.870		224.758		212.711	220.324			222.343		220.897
9T	Robby Gordon	94/L/F			214.388	217.019													
10	Mike Groff	94/L/H		219.159	211.238			220.783	218.346	220.033		212.791	219.947						
10T	Mike Groff	94/L/H		223.703	220.870	215.533	211.486	224.003	226.068	226.855	222.338	220.453							
11	Teo Fabi	94/R/IL			217.675	222.855	218.240						221.032	219.207	221.478		220.577	215.734	
11T	Teo Fabi	94/R/IL		215.218	215.900	217.250	217.239			219.566	220.399		221.266				222.173		218.606
12	Jacques Villeneuve	94/R/F			222.651	226.637		225.062	226.324	227.066	224.910	221.609	217.496	220.162	219.272				218.124
12T	Jacques Villeneuve	94/R/F						219.138							221.976	175.599	221.861	220.967	217.839
14	Bryan Herta	94/L/F			205.888							211.919			216.904	218.044			214.265
14T	Bryan Herta	94/L/F					213.093	217.607				215.208							
14T	Johnny Rutherford	94/L/F																	
15	Robby Gordon	94/L/F				219.320	214.051	219.197	218.235	219.582	211.755	222.327	219.947			217.507	221.038		204.601
15	Mark Smith	94/L/F			211.238							219.411			221.386				209.609
15T	Mark Smith	93/L/F		217.349	217.675	216.904	215.770	223.392	223.242	224.618	222.124	219.101	219.411	216.523	213.883			206.436	
16	Stefan Johansson	93/P/IL						214.777	223.070	219.566	220.399			219.528		193.569	206.744		
16T	Gary Bettenhausen	93/P/IL					192.567												
16T	Stefan Johansson	93/P/IL		218.161	219.010	220.275	218.055	225.462	222.745	225.598			217.496	220.162	219.272		221.861	220.967	218.124
17	Dominic Dobson	93/P/IL		179.404	221.457	222.728	223.303	224.781	226.803	224.500	224.910		221.686		221.976	175.599			217.839
18	Jimmy Vasser	94/R/F						222.069	224.562							208.836	210.349	212.590	205.573
18T	Jimmy Vasser	94/R/F		213.493	214.123	221.582	219.159	221.648	221.642	223.519				211.780		220.291		220.491	217.066
19	Brian Till	93/L/F		225.558	225.739	224.708	218.023	224.305	223.908	226.637				222.988					
21	Roberto Guerrero	92/L/B					220.919	223.070	220.897					219.528					210.285
21T	Roberto Guerrero	92/L/B		215.440	211.268	210.079	214.179	216.169	220.410	222.151		208.531	216.206	214.961	217.381				
22	Raul Boesel	94/L/F		219.416	220.550	208.889	215.198	217.475	218.537	217.881	219.320			216.357	220.070	219.609	220.227	217.391	
22	Hiro Matsushita	94/L/F						220.897				221.965				212.595	214.516	213.548	
23	Buddy Lazier	93/L/L			209.937	209.045	178.331	213.270	216.575	220.913	211.556		215.750					207.708	
24	Robby Gordon	94/L/F																	
24	Willy T. Ribbs	94/L/F																	
24T	Willy T. Ribbs	93/L/F																	

1994 DAILY BEST SPEEDS

Car	Driver	YR/CH/E	5/07	5/08	5/09	5/10	5/11	5/12	5/13	5/14	5/15	5/16	5/17	5/18	5/19	5/20	5/21	5/22	5/26
25	Marco Greco	94/L/F		206.275	206.564						216.092				220.108	217.607		203.883	203.952
25T	Marco Greco	93/L/F							217.865	215.326						218.436	221.304	221.751	221.315
27	Eddie Cheever	93/L/M		223.998	224.221	228.676		226.620	226.729	224.014								212.024	
27T	Scott Brayton	93/L/M									227.508							217.602	222.905
27T	Eddie Cheever	93/L/M			214.510		220.383			227.106									216.429
28	Arie Luyendyk	94/L/IL		216.476	217.623	222.063	214.905	225.983	223.875	225.293			213.960	221.457	222.140	224.243			
28T	Arie Luyendyk	94/L/IL		190.573					218.606						209.142				
30	Pancho Carter	93/L/IL											213.858	216.805	217.839				
30	Stephan Gregoire	93/L/IL																212.515	
30T	Pancho Carter	93/L/IL				211.253	209.531	216.383	216.779	215.172	214.941	212.998							
31	Paul Tracy	94/P/MB		217.244													217.439		218.050
31	Al Unser, Jr.	94/P/MB			223.897	226.085	226.478	227.457	227.359	229.481									
31T	Emerson Fittipaldi	94/P/MB					224.422										226.057		
31T	Paul Tracy	94/P/MB									224.159								218.468
31T	Al Unser, Jr.	94/P/MB				217.544			220.534										
33	John Andretti	94/L/F		201.780	213.427	222.365	221.544	222.519		224.310					218.771				213.589
39	Ross Bentley	93/L/F																	
40	Scott Goodyear	94/L/F		219.357	217.292	222.761	218.760	220.761	219.802	223.037			216.507	216.138	215.079	220.881	222.178	219.170	
40T	Scott Goodyear	94/L/F			221.724					225.762	222.091								216.601
40T	Davy Jones	94/L/F													212.119	217.155	224.361		
41T	Bryan Herta	93/L/F														223.408	205.667	222.932	213.756
42	Johnny Parsons	93/L/G		191.095						207.579	204.146		199.375						
44	Roberto Moreno	94/L/F												206.868	216.836	216.638	220.469	215.698	
44	Tero Palmroth	94/L/F				214.613	211.060	215.652	213.210	219.250	210.438								
44	Al Unser	94/L/F		191.249	192.066														
44T	Al Unser	93/L/F			205.705														
45	John Paul, Jr.	93/L/IL		218.198	220.475	222.063	200.723	221.239	220.637	223.109	220.432				218.452	221.691	223.048		207.934
46	John Paul, Jr.	93/L/IL												218.643	222.058	221.658	210.802		
50	Bobby Rahal	93/L/IL													224.143	225.536	226.102		215.822
51	Eddie Cheever	92/L/M					211.820												
52T	Mike Groff	93/P/IL											222.833	221.560	222.888	223.264	224.143		214.316
52T	Bobby Rahal	93/P/IL											215.833	219.657					
52T	Paul Tracy	93/P/IL													221.391		217.381		
59	Geoff Brabham	93/L/M									219.197		216.659	220.437		224.557			
59	Scott Brayton	93/L/M		227.658		226.529	220.691	224.573	227.003	221.457							220.340		
59T	Geoff Brabham	93/L/M															221.359		
59T	Scott Brayton	93/L/M			225.926	222.173				223.747									
59T	Eddie Cheever	93/L/M											210.832	221.185	223.775	219.288	223.010	217.623	
61	Gary Bettenhausen	93/P/IL				214.046	217.087	221.054	220.962	223.447					221.462	221.190			
64	Didier Theys	94/L/F														206.820	212.786	217.334	
71	Dominic Dobson	94/L/F		218.818	220.637	220.227	220.989	224.955	224.910	225.507									
71	Dominic Dobson	94/L/F																	
71T	Scott Sharp	94/L/F														217.045			
71T	Dominic Dobson	94/L/F																	217.339
71T	Scott Sharp	94/L/F																	
74	Jim Crawford	91/L/B		205.451	192.827	207.273					205.780	210.482	217.003	221.795	220.718	214.072	219.362	220.594	211.178
79	Dennis Vitolo	93/L/F		214.905	208.141		206.167	203.887	209.307			210.187	202.584		199.880		211.431	185.399	
88	Mauricio Gugelmin	94/R/F			211.924	219.421		217.223	219.448	222.954									
89	Mauricio Gugelmin	94/R/F					221.288	223.580	221.440	222.833				219.325	221.489	224.299	226.182		216.367
90	Lyn St. James	94/L/F		216.763	215.512	220.259	220.318	224.400	225.745	224.282		218.293	215.445	215.528	218.691				214.664
91	Stan Fox	94/R/F							220.459	225.242			217.628		216.534				211.183
94	Jeff Andretti	92/L/B		218.431	215.260	215.905	218.304	220.124						208.478	214.123	215.848	218.531	215.522	
94	Stan Fox	92/L/B																	
94	Buddy Lazier	92/L/B			211.974													220.567	
95	Stan Fox	93/L/B		214.57															
99	Hideshi Matsuda	94/L/F			218.489			220.318	221.566	222.646		220.723	217.912						216.518

1994 QUALIFICATION ATTEMPTS
CHRONOLOGICAL SUMMARY

QA	Time	Car	Driver	Lap-1	Lap-2	Lap-3	Lap-4	Four-Lap Average	SR	SP
Saturday May 14, 1994 - Pole Day										
1	12:15	99	Hideshi Matsuda	222.646	222.640	222.409	222.486	222.545	21	14
2	12:25	27	Eddie Cheever	223.236	223.380	223.303	222.734	223.163	15	11
3	12:30	59T	Scott Brayton	221.779	221.593	219.974	Waved off			
4	12:35	17	Dominic Dobson	223.597	223.353	222.211	222.723	222.970	17	12
5	12:46	40	Scott Goodyear	222.288	222.425	221.495	Waved off			
6	12:50	5	Raul Boesel	227.393	227.837	227.623	227.618	227.618	2	2
7	12:56	7	Adrian Fernandez	218.282	Waved off					
8	12:59	79	Dennis Vitolo	222.124	222.069	222.612	222.954	222.439	23	15
9	1:04	8	Michael Andretti	226.108	226.449	226.142	226.119	226.205	5	5
10	1:08	9	Robby Gordon	222.102	220.432	Waved off				
11	1:12	12	Jacques Villeneuve	226.313	227.061	226.142	225.524	226.259	4	4
12	1:18	31	Al Unser Jr.	225.722	228.351	228.525	229.481	228.011	1	1
13	1:24	11	Teo Fabi	220.973	Waved off					
14	1:28	10T	Mike Groff	218.362	218.606	219.085	219.181	218.808	38	
15	1:36	4	Bobby Rahal	220.302	220.173	220.065	220.173	220.178	37	
16	1:40	28	Arie Luyendyk	225.293	224.966	222.189	222.283	223.673	10	8
17	1:45	1	Nigel Mansell	224.579	224.691	223.602	223.297	224.041	8	7
18	1:49	91	Stan Fox	222.030	223.065	223.198	223.181	222.867	18	13
19	4:58	71	Scott Sharp	222.156	222.091	221.899	222.217	222.091	25	17
20	5:03	33	John Andretti	224.182	224.310	222.327	222.250	223.263	14	10
21	5:08	90	Lyn St. James	224.120	224.282	224.070	224.143	224.154	6	6
22	5:19	45	John Paul, Jr	218.420	220.286	220.729	Waved off			
23	5:24	19	Brian Till	220.453	222.200	220.946	220.837	221.107	32	21
24	5:28	59	Scott Brayton	220.924	221.108	Waved off				
25	5:32	44	Al Unser	214.225	Waved off					
26	5:36	14	Bryan Herta	218.829	221.943	221.555	221.669	220.992	33	22
27	5:39	11T	Teo Fabi	219.566	218. 409	Waved off				
28	5:45	88	Mauricio Gugelmin	222.783	220.286	219.630	219.175	220.460	36	
29	5:50	21	Roberto Guerrero	220.302	221.795	221.261	221.762	221.278	30	20
30	5:55	25	Marco Greco	214.531	215.326	Waved off				
31	5:58	22	Hiro Matsushita	220.783	222.085	222.151	220.518	221.382	27	18
Sunday, May 15, 1994										
32	12:45	6	Mario Andretti	225.457	222.261	223.608	222.712	223.503	12	9
33	12:49	40T	Scott Goodyear	216.461	218.272	Waved off				
34	12:54	24	Willy T. Ribbs	211.556	Waved off					
35	12:57	9T	Robby Gordon	220.448	221.713	221.402	221.615	221.293	29	19
36	1:05	16	Stefan Johansson	220.783	219.427	Waved off				
37	1:09	27T	Scott Brayton	223.021	Waved off					
38	1:13	18	Jimmy Vasser	222.513	222.607	222.107	221.822	222.262	24	16
39	1:18	2	Emerson Fittipaldi	227.987	227.061	227.198	226.969	227.303	3	3
End of First Day Qualifications										
40	1:30	31T	Paul Tracy	222.233	222.058	220.875	Waved off			
41	1:35	7T	Adrian Fernandez	222.607	222.217	222.855	222.949	222.657	20	26
42	2:34	31T	Paul Tracy	223.081	222.261	223.026	222.475	222.710	19	25
43	4:53	11	Teo Fabi	222.894	224.523	224.037	222.140	223.394	13	24
44	5:30	45	John Paul, Jr	219.861	219.748	219.357	Waved off			
45	5:45	27T	Scott Brayton	225.028	222.546	223.425	223.625	223.652	11	23
46	5:52	16	Stefan Johansson	221.817	221.664	221.893	220.702	221.518	26	27
47	5:57	23	Buddy Lazier	218.055	218.585	Waved off				
Saturday, May 21, 1994										
48	11:00	45	John Paul, Jr.	221.588	222.662	223.048	222.706	222.500	22	30
49	11:07	25T	Marco Greco	217.439	218.452	218.616	Waved off			
50	11:12	40	Scott Goodyear	221.244	220.534	221.049	220.124	220.737	34	
51	5:31	89	Mauricio Gugelmin (Withdrew the #88 car prior to run)	223.669	223.408	223.209	222.134	223.104	16	29
52	5:37	15	Mark Smith	220.027	220.967	221.038	220.702	220.683	35	
53	5:42	40T	Davy Jones* (Mike Groff withdraws the #10T car)	224.361	223.286	223.875	223.747	223.817	9	33
54	5:46	52T	Mike Groff (Bobby Rahal withdraws the #4 car)	222.058	221.119	221.054	221.190	221.355	28	31
55	5:51	50	Bobby Rahal (Bumps #15 Mark Smith)	224.652	224.523	224.059	223.148	224.094	7	28
56	5:54	44	Tero Palmroth	217.155	Waved off					
57	5:59	23	Buddy Lazier	218.087	Waved off					
Sunday, May 22, 1994										
58	5:35	25T	Marco Greco (Bumps #40 Scott Goodyear)	221.261	221.163	221.751	220.691	221.216	31	32
59	5:40	59T	Geoff Brabham	221.190	220.496	219.990	Waved off			
60	5:45	15T	Mark Smith	Accident in Turn #1						
61	5:52	61	Gary Bettenhausen	218.161	218.574	Waved off				
62	5:59	9	Willy T. Ribbs	216.206	212.942	Waved off				

*Scott Goodyear replaces Davy Jones

QA=Qualification Attempt   SR=Overall Speed Rank   SP=Starting Position

	CAR		DRIVER	CAR NAME	YR/C/E	TIME	SPEED
1	31	W	Al Unser, Jr.	Marlboro Penske Mercedes	94/P/MB	2:37.887	228.011
2	5		Raul Boesel	Duracell Charger	94/L/F	2:38.160	227.618
3	2	W	Emerson Fittipaldi	Marlboro Penske Mercedes	94/P/MB	2:38.379	227.303
4	12	R	Jacques Villeneuve	Player's LTD Forsythe-Green	94/R/F	2:39.110	226.259
5	8		Michael Andretti	Target/Scotch Video Chip Ganassi Racing	94/R/F	2:39.148	226.205
6	90		Lyn St. James	Spirit of the American Woman-JCPenney/Reebok/Lee	94L/F	2:40.604	224.154
7	1		Nigel Mansell	Kmart Texaco Havoline Newman-Haas Racing	94/L/F	2:40.685	224.041
8	28	W	Arie Luyendyk	Indy Regency Racing-Eurosport	93/L/IL	2:40.949	223.673
9	6	W	Mario Andretti	Kmart Texaco Havoline Newman-Haas Racing	94/L/F	2:41.072	223.503
10	33		John Andretti	A.J. Foyt/Jonathan Byrd's Cafeteria/Bryant	94/L/F	2:41.245	223.263
11	27		Eddie Cheever	Quaker State Special	93/L/M	2:41.317	223.163
12	17		Dominic Dobson	PacWest Racing	94/L/F	2:41.457	222.970
13	91		Stan Fox	Delta Faucet-Jack's Tool Rental-Hemelgarn Racing	94/R/F	2:41.531	222.867
14	99	R	Hideshi Matsuda	Beck Motorsports/Simon Racing	93/L/F	2:41.765	222.545
15	79	R	Dennis Vitolo	Hooligan's/Carlo/Charter America/Dick Simon Racing	93/L/F	2:41.842	222.439
16	18		Jimmy Vasser	Conseco-STP	94/R/F	2:41.971	222.262
17	71	R	Scott Sharp	PacWest Racing	94/L/F	2:42.096	222.091
18	22		Hiro Matsushita	Panasonic Duskin	94/L/F	2:42.615	221.382
19	9		Robby Gordon	Valvoline Cummins Ford	94/L/F	2:42.680	221.293
20	21		Roberto Guerrero	Interstate Batteries/Pagan Racing	92/L/B	2:42.691	221.278
21	19	R	Brian Till	The Mi-Jack Car	93/L/F	2:42.817	221.107
22	14	R	Bryan Herta	A.J. Foyt Copenhagen Racing	94/L/F	2:42.902	220.992
23	59		Scott Brayton	Glidden Paint Special	93/L/M	2:40.964	223.652
24	11		Teo Fabi	Pennzoil Special	94/R/IL	2:41.150	223.394
25	3		Paul Tracy	Marlboro Penske Mercedes	94/P/MB	2:41.645	222.710
26	7	R	Adrian Fernandez	Tecate/Quaker State/Reynard/Ilmor	94/R/IL	2:41.684	222.657
27	16		Stefan Johansson	Alumax Aluminum	93/P/IL	2:42.515	221.518
28	4	W	Bobby Rahal	Miller Genuine Draft	93/P/IL	2:40.647	224.094
29	88	R	Mauricio Gugelmin	Hollywood Indy Car Chip Ganassi Racing	94/R/F	2:41.360	223.104
30	45		John Paul, Jr.	CYBERGENICS/Team Losi/Pro Formance	93/L/IL	2:41.798	222.500
31	10		Mike Groff	Motorola	93/P/ILC+	2:42.635	221.355
32	25	R	Marco Greco	Int Sports LTD	94/L/F	2:42.737	221.216
33	40	*	Scott Goodyear	Budweiser King Racing	94/L/F	2:40.846	223.817

*Car originally qualified by Davy Jones in the 29th position

33-Car Field Average: 223.270 (1993: 219.692) Slower by 3.578 MPH

LEGEND:
Chassis: L=Lola, **P**=Penske, **R**=Reynard
Engines: B=Buick Indy V6, **F**=Ford Cosworth XB, **IL**=Ilmor V8-D, **ILC+**=Ilmor C+, **M**=Menard V6/B, **MB**=Mercedes Benz
W=Winner, **R**=Rookie

Car No.	Driver	SP	Lap 10	20	30	40	50	60	70	80	90	100	110	120	130	140	150	160	170	180	190	Finish 200	Laps Comp	Running or Reason Out
33	Andretti, John	10	10	10	6	5	3	5	13	10	9	9	9	7	8	12	12	12	12	12	11	10	196	Running
6	Andretti, Mario	9	5	4	31	32	32	32	32	32	32	32	32	32	32	32	32	32	32	32	32	32	23	Fuel Pump
8	Andretti, Michael	5	3	3	3	4	16	15	8	13	11	5	5	5	5	6	5	7	3	5	6	6	198	Running
5	Boesel, Raul	2	8	7	7	7	4	7	10	9	6	10	19	20	21	21	21	21	21	21	21	21	100	Water Pump
59	Brayton, Scott	23	18	18	14	13	8	8	6	6	10	5	6	16	19	19	20	20	21	21	20	20	116	Engine
27	Cheever, Eddie	11	6	5	4	3	14	12	16	12	13	11	10	8	10	8	8	11	8	10	8	8	197	Running
17	Dobson, Dominic	12	12	11	19	29	29	29	29	29	29	29	29	29	29	29	29	29	29	29	29	29	29	Accident
11	Fabi, Teo	24	17	17	17	16	15	13	11	15	15	12	11	10	11	9	9	8	7	8	7	7	198	Running
7	Fernandez, Adrian	26	22	21	15	26	27	28	28	28	28	28	28	28	28	28	28	28	28	28	28	28	30	Suspension
2	Fittipaldi, Emerson	3	2	2	1	1	1	1	1	1	1	1	1	1	1	1	1	1	1	1	13	17	184	Accident
91	Fox, Stan	13	13	12	13	14	12	11	19	17	17	13	12	11	12	11	10	10	9	9	10	13	193	Accident
40	Goodyear, Scott	33	31	32	29	30	30	30	30	30	30	30	30	30	30	30	30	30	30	30	30	30	29	Mechanical
9	Gordon, Robby	19	28	23	9	9	5	6	9	8	5	8	8	5	7	4	4	4	7	4	5	5	199	Running
25	Greco, Marco	32	33	33	28	21	25	25	26	27	27	27	27	27	27	27	27	27	27	27	27	27	53	Electrical
10	Groff, Mike	31	30	31	30	31	31	31	31	31	31	31	31	31	31	31	31	31	31	31	31	31	28	Accident
21	Guerrero, Roberto	20	19	20	33	33	33	33	33	33	33	33	33	33	33	33	33	33	33	33	33	33	20	Accident
88	Gugelmin, Mauricio	29	32	29	25	24	24	24	24	21	21	17	16	14	13	13	13	13	14	13	12	11	196	Running
14	Herta, Bryan	22	24	24	22	23	19	18	12	16	16	14	13	12	9	10	9	11	11	9	9	9	197	Running
16	Johansson, Stefan	27	26	26	20	17	17	16	21	18	18	15	14	13	14	13	16	17	17	17	16	15	192	Running
28	Luyendyk, Arie	8	4	9	10	10	10	20	15	22	22	16	15	15	17	15	15	15	14	14	17	18	179	Engine
1	Mansell, Nigel	7	7	6	5	6	13	10	7	7	3	20	21	22	22	22	22	22	22	22	22	22	92	Accident
99	Matsuda, Hideshi	14	15	15	12	12	11	9	14	11	7	22	23	24	24	24	24	24	24	24	24	24	90	Accident
22	Matsushita, Hiro	18	27	28	23	19	22	23	24	24	24	24	19	18	16	17	17	16	16	16	15	14	193	Running
45	Paul Jr., John	30	29	30	21	18	18	17	22	19	19	23	24	25	25	25	25	25	25	25	25	25	89	Accident
4	Rahal, Bobby	28	23	22	16	15	9	14	5	4	8	4	4	6	4	6	5	5	6	6	3	3	199	Running
90	St. James, Lyn	6	11	16	18	27	28	27	26	26	26	26	20	21	20	20	19	19	19	19	19	19	170	Running
71	Sharp, Scott	17	16	14	32	28	26	26	25	25	25	25	18	19	18	18	18	18	18	18	18	16	186	Running
19	Till, Brian	21	25	27	26	22	23	21	20	20	20	18	17	15	15	16	14	13	13	15	14	12	194	Running
3	Tracy, Paul	25	21	19	27	25	20	19	18	14	14	21	22	23	23	23	23	23	23	23	23	23	92	Turbocharger
31	Unser Jr., Al	1	1	1	2	2	2	2	2	2	2	2	2	2	3	3	2	2	2	2	1	1	200	Running
18	Vasser, Jimmy	16	14	13	8	8	6	4	4	5	12	7	7	4	6	7	7	6	6	7	4	4	199	Running
12	Villeneuve, Jacques	4	9	8	11	11	7	3	3	3	4	3	3	3	2	3	3	3	4	3	2	2	200	Running
79	Vitolo, Dennis	15	20	25	24	20	21	22	23	23	23	24	25	26	26	26	26	26	26	26	26	26	89	Accident

FP	SP	CAR		DRIVER	YR/CH/E	LAPS	TIME	SPEED	RUNNING/ REASON OUT	SPEEDWAY PRIZES	TOTAL PRIZES
1	1	31	W	Al Unser, Jr.	94/P/MB	200	3:06:29.006	160.872	Running	$878,900	$1,373,813
2	4	12	RY	Jacques Villeneuve	94/R/F	200	3:06:37.606	160.749	Running	441,700	622,713
3	28	4	W	Bobby Rahal	93/P/IL	199	3:06:34.301	159.992	Running	331,100	411,163
4	16	18		Jimmy Vasser	94/R/F	199	3:06:36.145	159.966	Running	215,600	295,163
5	19	9		Robby Gordon	94/L/F	199	3:06:36.455	159.961	Running	203,500	227,563
6	5	8		Michael Andretti	94/R/F	*198	3:06:33.498	159.200	Running	194,500	245,563
7	24	11		Teo Fabi	94/R/IL	198	3:06:40.098	159.106	Running	196,200	216,563
8	11	27		Eddie Cheever	93/L/M	197	3:06:32.827	158.405	Running	178,500	238,563
9	22	14	R	Bryan Herta	94/L/F	197	3:06:35.786	158.363	Running	171,700	212,213
10	10	33		John Andretti	94/L/F	196	3:06:35.053	157.570	Running	168,000	191,750
11	29	88	R	Mauricio Gugelmin	94/R/F	196	3:06:44.192	157.441	Running	169,500	182,063
12	21	19	R	Brian Till	93/L/F	194	3:06:43.025	155.851	Running	161,200	180,763
13	13	91		Stan Fox	94/R/F	193	3:00:18.801	160.554	Accident	158,000	186,313
14	18	22		Hiro Matsushita	94/L/F	193	3:06:39.297	155.099	Running	154,700	177,013
15	27	16		Stefan Johansson	93/P/IL	192	3:06:38.668	154.304	Running	151,800	164,113
16	17	71	R	Scott Sharp	94/L/F	186	3:06:30.170	149.596	Running	149,100	161,663
17	3	2	W	Emerson Fittipaldi	94/P/MB	184	2:44:21.741	167.922	Accident	146,600	298,163
18	8	28	W	Arie Luyendyk	94/L/IL	179	2:45:56.398	161.806	Engine	144,100	161,412
19	6	90		Lyn St. James	94/L/F	170	3:06:41.737	136.586	Running	141,900	161,212
20	23	59		Scott Brayton	93/L/M	116	1:58:41.719	146.594	Engine	164,800	177,112
21	2	5		Raul Boesel	94/L/F	100	1:41:55.170	147.175	Water Pump	137,800	173,112
22	7	1		Nigel Mansell	94/L/F	92	1:26:18.585	159.889	Accident	136,000	153,312
23	25	3		Paul Tracy	94/P/MB	92	1:36:40.697	142.741	Turbocharger	139,300	151,612
24	14	99	R	Hideshi Matsuda	93/L/F	90	1:25:19.161	158.229	Accident	132,800	150,362
25	30	45		John Paul, Jr.	93/L/IL	89	1:25:37.576	155.910	Accident	131,500	168,812
26	15	79	R	Dennis Vitolo	93/L/F	89	1:26:33.261	154.238	Accident	130,300	143,862
27	32	25	R	Marco Greco	94/L/F	53	1:34:59.114	83.697	Electrical	154,200	171,762
28	26	7	R	Adrian Fernandez	94/R/IL	30	28:53.357	155.767	Suspension	128,300	146,612
29	12	17		Dominic Dobson	94/L/F	29	27:52.185	156.083	Accident	127,600	139,912
30	33	40		Scott Goodyear	94/L/F	29	30:02.121	144.829	Mechanical	137,000	159,312
31	31	10		Mike Groff	93/P/ILC+	28	27:52090	150.710	Accident	126,500	138,812
32	9	6	W	Mario Andretti	94/L/F	23	19:38.803	175.602	Fuel System	126,200	138,512
33	20	21		Roberto Guerrero	92/L/B	20	16:35.795	180.760	Accident	126,100	143,912

TOTAL: (1)$6,255,000 (1)$7,864,800

TIME OF RACE:	**3** Hours, 6 Minutes, 29.006 Seconds
AVERAGE SPEED:	160.872 MPH
FASTEST LAP OF RACE:	#2 Fittipaldi, Lap 121: 220.680 MPH
FASTEST LEADING LAP:	Lap 121, Fittipaldi
MARGIN OF VICTORY:	8.6 Seconds

LAP LEADERS: Emerson Fittipaldi, $62,250 (145 laps: 24-61, 64-124, 130-133, 139-164, 169-184); Al Unser, Jr., $21,600 (48 laps: 1-23, 134-138, 165-168, 185-200); Jacques Villeneuve, $3,150 (7 laps: 62-63, 125-129).

Legend: FP=Finish Position, **SP**=Start Position, **W**=Former Winner, **R**=Rookie, **RY**=Rookie of the Year **Chassis Legend: L**=Lola, **P**=Penske, **R**=Reynard
Engine Legend: B=Buick Indy V6,, **F**=Ford Cosworth XB, **IL**=Ilmor V8-D, **ILC+**=Ilmor C+, **M**=Menard, **MB**=Mercedes Benz V8
1) All-time Records for: Speedway Total Purse and Total Overall Purse ***=Penalties

LAP PRIZE LEADERS

1	Emerson Fittipaldi**	$227,250
2	Mario Andretti*	199,350
3	Michael Andretti	151,650
4	Rick Mears****	144,450
5	Al Unser****	123,200
6	A.J. Foyt, Jr****	97,716
7	Bobby Unser***	82,597
8	Parnelli Jones*	75,050
9	Danny Sullivan*	72,900
10	Gordon Johncock**	67,273

TOTAL MONEY WINNERS

1	Rick Mears****	$4,299,392
2	Al Unser, Jr.**	4,262,690
3	Emerson Fittipaldi**	4,042,767
4	Al Unser****	3,378,018
5	Arie Luyendyk*	2,995,259
6	Mario Andretti*	2,766,931
7	A.J. Foyt, Jr.****	2,637,963
8	Bobby Rahal*	2,416,329
9	Michael Andretti	2,095,868
10	Danny Sullivan*	1,870,756

LAP LEADERS

1	Al Unser****	644
2	Ralph DePalma*	612
3	Mario Andretti*	556
4	A.J. Foyt, Jr****	555
5	Wilbur Shaw***	508
6	Emerson Fittipaldi**	505
7	Parnelli Jones*	492
8	Bill Vukovich**	485
9	Bobby Unser***	440
10	Rick Mears****	429

MILEAGE LEADERS

1	A.J. Foyt, Jr****	12,272.5
2	Al Unser****	10,890
3	Gordon Johncock**	7,895
4	Mario Andretti*	7,625
5	Johnny Rutherford***	6,980
6	Bobby Unser***	6,527.5
7	Cliff Bergere	6,145
8	Lloyd Ruby	6,097.5
9	Mauri Rose***	6,040
10	Rick Mears****	5,855

NUMBER OF RACES

1	A.J. Foyt, Jr****	35
2	Mario Andretti*	29
3	Al Unser****	27
4	Johnny Rutherford***	24
5	Gordon Johncock**	24
6	George Snider	22
7	Gary Bettenhausen	21
8	Bobby Unser***	19
9	Lloyd Ruby	18
10	Roger McCluskey	18
11	Tom Sneva*	18

500 POINT LEADERS

1	Al Unser****	11,000
2	A.J. Foyt, Jr****	10,190
3	Rick Mears****	7,375
4	Gordon Johncock**	6,910
5	Wilbur Shaw***	6,370
6	Bobby Unser***	6,170
7	Ted Horn	6,000
8	Louis Meyer***	5,784
9	Mauri Rose***	5,581
10	Al Unser, Jr.**	5,550

June, 1994

Each * = One Indy 500 Win

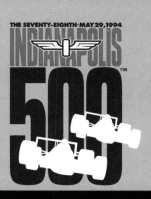

Alley, Jay   30
Altenschulte, Ray   43, 88
Binkley, Mag   23, 58, 73, 100, 103, 108
Boyd, Dan   4-5, 22, 33, 76, 80, 84, 86, 98-99
Edelstein, Dave   24, 51, 61, 90
Ellis, Steve   89
Fennig, Jim   11, 31, 47, 50, 62, 70, 87, 94
Haines, Jim   13, 28, 37, 40, 87, 91, 107, 109,
   Back Cover
Hunter, Harlen   41, 44, 45, 105
Hunter, Todd   58, 86, 112
Jones, Darryl   Inside Front Cover, 20, 24, 25, 30,
   40, 43, 48, 51, 52, 54, 60, 62, 72, 74, 79, 84, 85,
   86, 87, 88, 101, 102, 110
Kuhn, Walt   49, 92-93
Lawrence, Jerry   31, 41, 44, 45, 81, 87, 127
Lee, David   39
McManus, Steve   12, 44-45, 59, 77
McQueeney, Linda   13, 17, 18, 19, 33, 35, 36, 42,
   46, 49, 56, 82, 84, 85, 106, 111, 113
McQueeney, Ron   11, 14, 15, 16, 21, 23, 26, 30,
   32, 35, 40, 42, 43, 53, 56, 57, 61, 63, 64, 65, 67,
   68, 69, 71, 73, 75, 77, 78, 79, 80, 83, 85, 86, 88,

89, 91, 97, 99, Inside Back Cover
Reed, Mark   15, 31, 75, 82, 103
Scott, Bob   19, 91
Scott, Sam   28, 69, 91
Simmons, Elwood   20
Smith, Larry   17, 47, 55, 74, 78, 95, 105
Snoddy, Steve   36, 97, 102
Spargur, Leigh   15, 19, 53, 63, 66, 86, 90
Swope, Steve   Front Cover, 13, 14, 17, 21, 22, 25,
   29, 32, 34, 38, 55, 59, 60, 64, 70, 71, 72, 81, 83,
   84, 85, 87, 104, 109
Taylor, Pat   38
Totten Spivey, Kay   65, 68
Willoughby, Dave   27, 57
Young, Debbie   28, 33, 67, 90
Young, Loretta   96
Young, Mike   10, 29, 88, 89

Contributing photographers:
Indianapolis Motor Speedway   30, 37, 43
Indy Festivals, Inc.   44-45

**Cover portrait of Al Unser, Jr. by
Indiana artist Bill Rader**

Below indicate servicemarks and trademarks of the Indianapolis Motor Speedway Corporation, USA which reserves all rights thereto.

INDIANAPOLIS 500®

THE GREATEST SPECTACLE IN RACING®

INDY 500®

GASOLINE ALLEY®

THE BRICKYARD™

THE INDY®

HOME OF THE 500®

TRADITION

BRICKYARD
400®

THE
GREATEST
RACE COURSE
IN THE
WORLD®

BRICKYARD
CROSSING™

BRICKYARD
CROSSING
CHAMPIONSHIP™

INDY®

INDYCAR™

TRACKSIDE™

FORMULA
INDY™